MEDITERRANEAN DIET COOKBOOK

FOR BEGINNERS

The Complete Mediterranean Diet Guide to Kick Start A Healthy Lifestyle

Top 10 Success Tips

28 Days

Meal Plan

ROSE KISER

Table Of Content

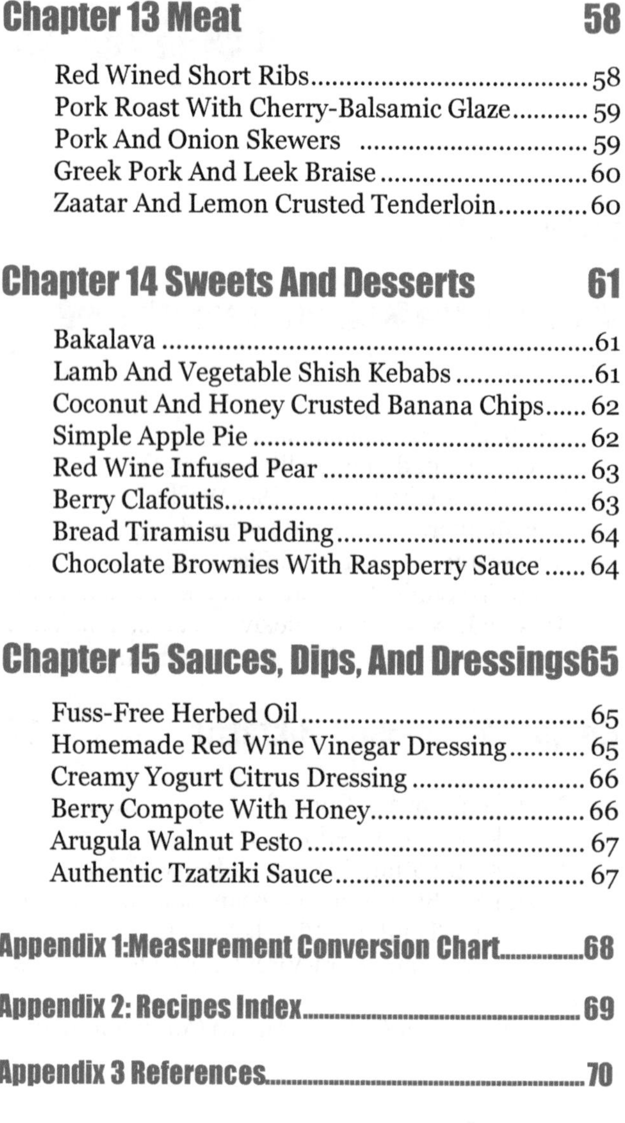

Introduction

I used to visit my grandmother every school holiday. It was during this time that I learned the value of eating healthily. Our plates would always look colorful, filled with either fruit or vegetables. My favorite was Grandma's fish dish. She would add olive oil to a frying pan and grill the fish fillets until golden. The smell of spinach, purple onion, garlic, and grape tomatoes filled the air while sautéing. When ready, this bright red mix would complement a serving of her tender fish. I only later realized that she was following the Mediterranean Diet. I don't think she even knew what it was called. To her, it was just about showing her love by cooking her family a healthy meal.

Now that I have three kids, I am very thankful that my grandma imparted her culinary knowledge to me. When I put the name "Mediterranean Diet" to her healthy lifestyle, I did some extensive research, and today I am able to provide my kids with wholesome, delicious food that will keep them in good physical shape.

I am proud to say that my family and I have overcome the attraction of over-processed, sugary foods. Instead of getting in the car and going to the nearest drive-through, we take the time to prepare healthy meals together. What is better than family time spent cooking wholesome, nutritious food that is beneficial to your longevity? The best yet is my kids never complain about eating their vegetables. They grew up appreciating what nature has to offer and will choose that over mass-produced plastic food.

In this cookbook, I will tell you more about the Mediterranean Diet and why it is so popular that doctors and dieticians all over the world recommend it. I will share with you my tips to start and stay on the Mediterranean Diet, but I will also tell you about some mistakes I made and how to avoid them. To help you, I will add a shopping list that contains the staples needed to ensure your success. It can be dangerous if you walk into a grocery store without a clear guide in hand. The temptation to buy unhealthy, processed foods is so much higher if you don't know what the healthy options are.

In the first two chapters, you will learn about the origins of the Mediterranean Diet and how it's not a diet in the traditional sense of the word. Although you will lose weight while eating delicious food, eating the Mediterranean way is about more than weight loss. It is about a healthy body and mind. I will also break down the basics of this diet, covering what foods you may eat and how much. You'll be happy to learn that very few foods are banned outright except for the synthetic, overly processed, and toxic kinds.

The recipes I include in this book will help you understand the Mediterranean food pyramid without being overly complex. That's one thing I want you to take away from this book; you won't need to follow complicated recipes or spend three hours a day in the kitchen to eat healthily. If you know the basics of which foods are good for you and why, and the foods to avoid, you'll be able to make the meals as intricate or simple as you see fit.

I hope this book helps you close the pantry door on the standard American diet and instead choose to nourish your body with hearty and wholesome foods. I know you can do it if you put your mind to it, and your whole body will thank you for choosing to take care of it.

Here's to you and your health!

Chapter 1: The Mediterranean Diet and Lifestyle

The Basics Concept

The Mediterranean Diet can be summarized as a balance of foods rich in antioxidants and healthy fats, and high in fiber. But I will go even further. It also focuses on spending time with loved ones while preparing and enjoying meals, self-control, exercising, and reducing stress. That is where the lifestyle part comes in, caring for all aspects of your life as a whole.

One thing I am very relieved about is that the Mediterranean Diet does not ask you to count calories, work out your macronutrients, or weigh your food. You will have to determine if the amount you are eating is within moderation or not. I know this may sound difficult to some, especially if you're overweight and struggle with binge eating. But you will soon realize that if you feed your body with wholesome food, you will feel better physically and emotionally, and in the end, will instinctively eat less.

The roots of the Mediterranean Diet date back to the Middle Ages, where it was enjoyed by rich and poor alike. Of course, the more affluent Greeks and Romans were not limited to salty fish, olives, and bread. They could enjoy oysters, other seafood, and a more extensive selection of fruits and vegetables. It's for this reason that people will argue that the Mediterranean Diet, in essence, evolved from a poor man's diet.

The benefits of this way of eating were discovered in the 1950s (Altomare et al., 2013). Dr. Ancel Keys and his colleagues were dumbfounded when they found that the underprivileged living in small towns across southern Italy were healthier than the affluent New Yorkers. Even their family members who had emigrated years before were sicklier than those who still lived in Italy. The Mediterranean Basin was yet to experience the arrival of fast food. Keys attributed the health of the area's people to simple, clean, and wholesome eating.

He went on to lead the Seven Countries Study, where he found a link between lifestyle, nutrition, and cardiovascular disease (Keys et al., 1986). Those eating the Mediterranean way had lower cholesterol and, consequently, better heart health. The abundant use of olive oil and eating more vegetables than meat had a positive effect on people's well-being.

The studies connecting the Mediterranean Diet with improved health aren't limited to only the 1950s. Many scientists have since examined how consuming mainly fruits, vegetables, whole grains, beans, and nuts can profoundly impact not only a person's heart but overall health.

Let's have a look at more recent studies that examine how eating the Mediterranean way can be beneficial to you.

Science Behind the Mediterranean Diet

Throughout the years, research has shown just how effective the Mediterranean Diet is in reducing the risk of not only cardiovascular diseases but also overall mortality rates (Trichopoulou, 2001).

But why is it that the Mediterranean Diet lowers cholesterol and, subsequently, the risk of cardiovascular disease while the standard American diet increases cholesterol and causes a large number of other deadly ailments?

If you consider that the average American diet involves eating large amounts of sodium, saturated fat, sugar, and refined carbohydrates in place of vegetables, fruits, and whole grains, the answer should be clear. It is no wonder that just over 42 percent of adults in the States are obese, and one in five children struggle with their weight (Centers for Disease Control and Prevention, 2015).

Those are some scary figures, and it is for this specific reason that doctors have started to recommend the Mediterranean Diet to their overweight patients all over the world. A diet encouraging you to pass up refined carbohydrates, processed foods, sugar, and unhealthy fats will, without a doubt, lead to weight loss and prevent weight-related illnesses like diabetes.

The diet's advantages, however, aren't limited to heart health and weight management. Studies have found that the diet has a positive impact on the cognitive abilities of the elderly (American Geriatrics Society, 2017). Without getting too technical, the stress and inflammation caused by eating over-processed, hormone-laden foods that contain saturated fat contribute to age-related diseases. A diet high in antioxidants can reverse cell stress as well as lower inflammation. Lucky for us, the Mediterranean Diet is packed full of foods high in just that – antioxidants.

Furthermore, women who follow the Mediterranean lifestyle are less likely to suffer from chronic diseases linked to old age (Trichopoulou et al., 2001). This includes type two diabetes, cancer, kidney disease, and lung disease.

As if the above isn't reason enough to start eating the Mediterranean way, this diet was recommended as a model for sustainable living (Food and Agricultural Organization of the United Nations, 2010). Since the diet limits animal foods, especially red meat, its environmental impact is reduced significantly. There's no mass food production, transportation, and consumption to add to the carbon emissions. The vegetables, fruits, and other plant-based foods eaten as part of this diet are usually local organic produce, and this also eliminates the use of plastic that only ends up in our oceans.

By now, it should be apparent just how much the Mediterranean Diet can help you, your loved ones, and the planet! You must be just as excited as I was when I first learned what value this lifestyle could add to my life. Let me break down the fundamentals so that I can get you one step closer to living a happier and longer life.

Why the Mediterranean Diet Works?

Losing weight is easy to do when it's stripped down to the basics. It's all about how much energy you take in versus how much you use during the day. For example, if you eat 3200 calories a day, but you have a desk job and don't exercise at all, your base metabolic rate (how many calories you need to keep your body going) will be low.

For argument's sake, let's say your BMR ends up at 2400 at the end of the day. That means you have overshot your energy needs by 800 calories. It may not sound like a lot, but if it happens every day throughout the week, you would have eaten 5600 more calories than you need to maintain your current body weight. Since one pound equals about 3500 calories, you would most likely gain one pound that week with the remaining 2100 going towards next week's calories (Mayo Clinic, n.d.). Should you then continue to fuel your body with more than you need, the pounds will keep packing on. It's basic math, really.

Of course, other factors play a role, such as your age, build, metabolism, and hormones if you're a woman.

So, how can the Mediterranean Diet help you achieve your dreams of a slimmer body?

Well, for a start, the diet requires you to limit processed and sugary foods that are high in calories. Just making this small change will already help you get your calorie intake under control.

Another contributing factor is the healthy fats you'll be eating daily. I know we've been told over and over again that fat makes you fat. To that, I say nonsense, and I have the science to back me! A group of doctors decided to compare weight loss results between low-carb, Mediterranean, and low-fat diets (Shai, 2008). They discovered that those who followed the Mediterranean Diet lost more weight than those on a low-fat diet. Better yet, they maintained their weight loss afterward.

The fact of the matter is that fat makes you feel fuller for longer, and when you're sated, gone is the temptation to stick your hand in the cookie jar! Talking about cookies, the healthy fats combined with the protein you'll be consuming while on the Mediterranean Diet will keep your glucose level in check. This means you won't get those nagging cravings for sugary foods.

If you're still not convinced that the Mediterranean Diet will have a positive effect on your weight, what if I told you that it helps pregnant women maintain their weight and may prevent obesity in children (Fernandes-Barres, 2016)? The evidence weighs in favor of trying the Mediterranean Diet to lose weight, wouldn't you say?

But there's more to it. As you now know, the Mediterranean Diet is a lifestyle.

Not only will you lose weight because you're eating wholesome foods, exercising and managing stress will also contribute to the fat melting away. You can imagine that this won't happen overnight. You will have to make a conscious decision to choose what goes into your mouth, as well as how you look after your body and mind in other ways.

The Mediterranean Food Pyramid

A helpful illustration of what you're allowed to eat, how much, and how often is the food pyramid. I particularly like the fact that social aspects like eating with your family and physical activity make up the foundation of the pyramid. It just drives home the point that the Mediterranean Diet is not just a way of eating; it is a way of living.

The pyramid is divided proportionally into groups containing foods you can choose from. The base, as I mentioned, is the lifestyle aspect. However, I adjusted the other levels somewhat. That is because, in addition to trusting the Mediterranean Diet, I also feel that limiting carbohydrate intake will have a noteworthy impact on your overall health.

Before we move on to the other tiers on the food pyramid, let me explain why carbohydrates may be harming your body.

First, let me make it clear that I am not against all carbs. Carbohydrates are essential sources of energy and nutrition. My issue lies with the simple carbs that make up so much of an American plate nowadays. Loaves of bread baked with white flour, heaps of sugar, soda, sweets, cookies, doughnuts, cake, all the things that we so quickly become addicted to. They jolt our blood sugar to high heaven and then crash just as fast.

This increase and drop of blood sugar play havoc on your insulin levels, and this can lead to insulin resistance and diabetes.

Complex carbohydrates like whole grains and oatmeal, on the other hand, are perfectly fine to eat. This form of carbohydrates gets broken down at a slower rate and will not cause your blood sugar to spike. It will also make you feel fuller for longer.

Considering the negative effects of simple carbs, I suggest limiting bread, pasta, rice, and products made with flour to only a few times a month. In contrast, the original pyramid states you can eat it daily.

Now that you know what slight modifications I suggest, I can break down the levels for you.

After the foundation tier, you get your fruits, vegetables, grains, beans, nuts, legumes, seeds, herbs and spices, olive oil, and other good fats. You can eat foods on this tier every day. Then you get your fish, seafood, poultry, eggs, and dairy. Limit this row to three to five times a week, and keep the poultry, eggs, and dairy portions small when you do eat them. Lastly and in this case also the least, we have meat, potatoes, rice, pasta, flour products, and sweets.

Let's have a closer look at the foods you may and may not eat.

Mediterranean Diet Pyramid

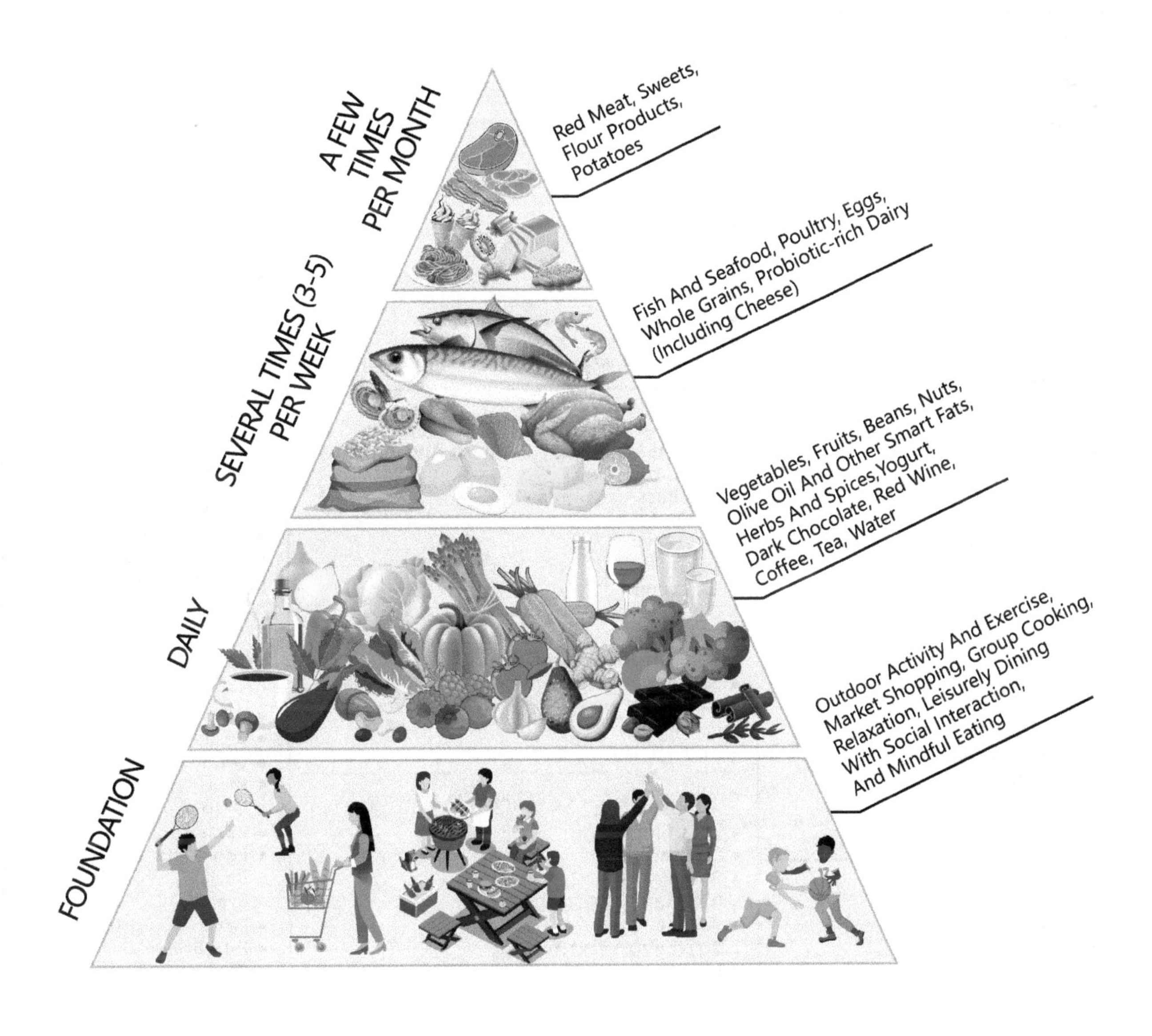

Mediterranean Diet Food List

FOODS TO EAT

OLIVE OIL, OLIVES, VINEGAR
- Extra-virgin Olive Oil
- Avocado Oil
- Olives
- Balsamic Vinegar
- Red Wine Vinegar

VEGETABLES
- Onions
- Garlic
- Potatoes
- Artichokes
- Zucchini
- Eggplant
- Squash
- Cucumbers
- Broccoli
- Cauliflower
- Mushrooms
- Beets
- Carrots
- Celery
- Peppers
- Fennel
- Cabbage
- Leeks
- Frozen

(Spinach, Peas, Green Beans)

NUTS AND SEEDS
- Pine Nuts
- Hazelnuts
- Walnuts
- Cashews
- Almonds
- Chestnuts
- Sesame Seeds
- Pumpkin Seeds
- Sunflower Seeds
- Tahini

GREENS
- Spinach
- Arugula
- Lettuce
- Kale
- Purslane
- Broccoli Rabe
- Beet Greens
- Collard Greens
- Dandelion Greens
- Mustard Greens
- Turnip Greens
- Chicory
- Dadelion
- Amaranth

HERBS AND SPICES
- Parsley
- Oregano
- Basil
- Dill
- Rosemary
- Mint
- Bay Leaves
- Salt
- Pepper
- Cumin
- Ginger
- Turmeric
- Saffron
- Paprika
- Cinnamon
- Cloves
- Red Pepper
- Flakes
- All Spice
- Nutmeg
- Herbal Teas

(Chamomile, Mountain Tea, Sage, Thyme)

FISH AND SEAFOOD
- Sardines (Fresh Or Canned) And Anchovies
- Salmon
- Sea Bass
- Halibut
- Tuna
- Trout
- Mackerel
- Oysters
- Crab
- Mussels And Clams
- Shrimps And Prawns
- Octopus
- Calamari
- Cod

CHEESE AND FERMENTED DAIRY
- Feta Cheese
- Mozzarella
- Parmesan
- Ricotta
- Yogurt
- Strained(Greek) Yogurt
- Milk Yogurt
- Graviera
- Mitzithra

MEAT AND POULTRY
- Grass Fed Beef
- Grass Fed Pork
- Grass Fed Chicken
- Organic Eggs
- Turkey
- Veal

FRUITS
- Grapes
- Tomatoes
- Lemons
- Oranges
- Grapefruit
- Apricots
- Applespears
- Pomegranate
- Cherries
- Avocado
- Watermelon
- Honeydew
- Peaches
- Strawberries
- Figs
- Kiwi
- Tangerines
- Cantaloupe
- Dates

BEANS AND LEGUMES
- Lentils
- Split Peas
- Broad Beans
- Chickpeas
- Kidney Beans
- Green Beans
- Black Beans
- Black Eyed Beans
- White Beans
- Pulses

WHOLE GRAINS, RICE, PASTA AND BREADS
- Whole Wheat
- Bulgur Wheat
- Quinoa
- Rice
- Orzo
- Pasta
- Egg Pasta
- Barley
- Bread
- Paximadi(Barley Rusks)
- Pita Bread
- Phyllo
- Rye
- Couscous

DRINKS
- Water
- Coffee
- Tea
- Wine
- Moonshine
- Fresh Juice

Most of the meals in the Mediterranean Diet are plant-based. It usually contains a generous helping of vegetables or a salad packed with anything from greens and arugula to roasted peppers. You will only find animal protein on your plate three to five days of the week. Fish and seafood will make up the bulk of your meat, but poultry is allowed too, although in smaller portions.

As you can see, this diet promotes eating colorful and fresh plant-based foods. Animal protein takes the back seat in the Mediterranean Diet, which stands wholly in contrast with the standard American diet. If we have a look at an American plate, you will see that animal protein is the main component with a starchy side coming in a close second. I would even go as far as to say it is a 50/50 split. Vegetables and salad, unfortunately, act only as a garnish. You may think I am overexaggerating, but if you think about it, you'll see it's the truth – or very close to it.

Add to that the fact that most American families live only on take-aways or frozen meals filled with artificial flavors, sodium, preservatives, and who knows what else. No wonder high cholesterol, hypertension, and diabetes are part of the top 10 reasons that Americans visit the doctor (Finley et al. 2018).

Following the Mediterranean Diet, vegetables, fruits, good fats, beans, nuts, yogurt (or even better yet, kefir), herbs and spices, coffee, tea, dark chocolate, and red wine will be your everyday essentials.

Yes, you read correctly – dark chocolate! You don't have to suffer when following this way of eating. You do, however, have to stop yourself from overindulging. Moderation is one of the critical points in the Mediterranean Diet.

Well, not so much when it comes to vegetables. You're more than welcome to eat your fill of vegetables and beans. Veggies are pretty substantial, and you will naturally stop eating when you're full. You will see that it is more challenging to eat the recommended five to nine servings of fruits and vegetables than it is to overeat.

Before I move on to the foods in the bad bin, let's break down the good.

Fresh Fruits and Vegetables

We all know that fruits and vegetables are full of vitamins and minerals, fiber, and complex carbohydrates. The skins are exceptionally healthy since they contain phytonutrients that fight diseases and contribute to your overall well-being.

A tip I can give you is to choose as many colors as you can. This way, you can be sure that you're eating a variety of phytonutrients and antioxidants, which will counteract free radicals. Go ahead and stack your plate with the colors of the rainbow. You'll find a pot of health at the end of it!

Colorful is the way to go when you eat the Mediterranean way.

Olive Oil

Olives contain monounsaturated fat which is extremely advantageous for your heart. Using olive oil instead of margarine or butter also lowers your chances of heart disease, cancer, and diabetes. This wonder oil also combats inflammatory disorders such as asthma and arthritis.

Another benefit of eating olive oil that is often overlooked is its role as a weight loss aid. This is primarily due to monounsaturated fat making you feel satiated for longer. If you make olive oil an integral part of your weight-loss regime, you are also more likely to stick to it since you won't feel deprived.

Fish

Although the positive impact of oily fish on one's health is well-documented, the importance this animal protein plays in providing us with adequate amounts of omega-3 fatty acids cannot be understated.

A staggering 90% of Americans are said to have an omega-3 deficiency (Thuppal et al. 2017). The changes in food production and transportation are mainly to blame. Consider the time before the Industrial Revolution when foods were organically grown by a local farmer in nutrient-rich soil, then bought and transported only a few miles to your home. Even the cattle had access to sources of omega-3 fat while freely roaming around, looking for a patch of grass to gnaw on.

Nowadays, produce is grown in nutrient-depleted soil and transported miles and miles to reach grocery stores, which means the use of preservatives is a necessity. Cattle are kept in feedlots where they can't even turn around comfortably and injected with hormones and antibiotics that are harmful to our gut microflora.

The end result is a diet devoid of naturally occurring omega-3 fat. This is worrying because as anti-inflammatory omega-3 ingestion decreases, there is nothing to offset the pro-inflammatory omega-6. Ideally, the omega-3/omega-6 ratio should be 1/1; in America, it is somewhere between 1/10 and 1/20. With this imbalance comes:

- Acne
- Arthritis
- Cancer
- Depression
- Allergies
- Asthma
- Heart disease
- Diabetes
- Hypertension
- Inflammatory bowel syndrome

The Mediterranean Diet includes ample intake of omega-3 fatty acids and limits the volume of omega-6 fatty acids.

A word of caution: Fish contain high levels of mercury which may be dangerous to pregnant women and children. Fish high in omega-3 usually contain less mercury. Salmon, sea bass, herring, sardines, flounder, trout, shad, and pollock are all great choices. Avoid shark, swordfish, tilefish, and king mackerel

Nuts

Almonds and walnuts aren't only rich in monounsaturated fat and omega-3 fatty acids; they also contain vitamins and fiber and are a brilliant source of protein.

What I enjoy most about nuts is how they fight the hunger pangs you may feel during the day. It only takes a few nuts to see you over to your next meal.

Of course, the evidence that nuts fight bad cholesterol, keep your triglyceride levels under control, make the lining of your arteries stronger, and prevent blood clots from forming are also reasons that I love nuts (Mayo Clinic, n.d.).

Beans or Legumes

Regularly consuming beans reduces your risk of getting cancer and diabetes, and it also lowers the risk of heart disease. Beans are fiber-rich, which means you will stay fuller for longer. It doesn't matter if you eat beans, chickpeas, lentils, or peas. All legumes have a cholesterol-lowering effect (Nierenberg, 2014).

Whole Grains

Oatmeal, quinoa, barley, and kasha are common non-refined grains used in the Mediterranean Diet. What makes whole grains superior to refined grains is the fact that all three layers are intact. The fiber, complex carbs and protein, and vitamins and minerals are undamaged.

The refining process strips the outer fibrous layer or both the outer and vitamin-rich layers. Don't think that because refined grains contain fewer ingredients it means fewer calories. The refining process actually bumps up the calorie content, meaning you'll be eating something with a lot less nutritional value but with more calories. Not worth the payoff if you ask me.

Red Wine

I am going to preface this by reminding you of the moderation principle of the Mediterranean Diet, so you shouldn't get too happy in thinking you can continue drinking a bottle of red. You should not consume more than two, 5-ounce glasses of red wine per day.

Moderate consumption of red wine as part of a balanced diet lowers bad cholesterol (LDD) while raising good cholesterol (HDL). This is thanks to the polyphenols and resveratrol contained in red wine. These two power substances are also linked to heart health and prevent blood clots from forming.

Dark Chocolate

Dark chocolate is jam-packed with potent antioxidants called flavanols, which help to maintain your blood sugar levels, fight bad cholesterol, and lower blood pressure.

You don't have to pull your sweet tooth.

Foods to Limit or Avoid

ADDED SUGAR	REFINED OILS
• Soda • Candies • Ice Cream • Table Sugar And Many Others	• Soybean Oil • Canola Oil • Cottonseed Oil And Others
REFINED GRAINS	**PROCESSED MEAT**
• White Bread • Pasta Made With Refined Wheat • Etc	• Processed Sausages • Hot Dogs • Etc
TRANS FATS	**HIGHLY PROCESSED FOODS**
• Found In Margarine And Various Processed Foods	• Anything Labeled "Low-fat" Or "Diet" Or Which Looks Like It Was Made In A Factory.

I mentioned earlier that no foods are forbidden from the Mediterranean Diet unless it is harmful to your overall health. While we all know we should pass up on consuming sugary foodstuffs such as candy, the majority of people are still unaware that high-fructose corn syrup is worse than regular table sugar. Found in all kinds of products, including soda, energy drinks, and boxed cookies, this sweetener plays havoc on your body's internal processes (Bray, 2013).

Fructose has no influence on our energy needs. It gets sent straight to the liver. This puts a lot of strain on your liver since it has to convert these unused calories into triglyceride, which is stored in your fat cells. If the triglyceride storage gets too large, it increases your risk of heart disease.

The next food item I want you to limit or avoid entirely if you can is milk. I think the benefits of drinking three glasses of milk a day have been overplayed in the standard American diet. It has been a significant player in the obesity epidemic taking America by storm.

Consuming so much full cream milk will predictably increase your cholesterol due to the high saturated fat content. Furthermore, it is never a good idea to drink your calories. Considering that the recommended daily intake has 450 calories, you can imagine how easy it is to overshoot your calorie limit to maintain a healthy weight.

If you have to drink milk, instead select fat-free or almond milk, and practice self-control when you want to overindulge. The same goes for cheese and yogurt – fat-free is best.

Last on my list is red meat. Overeating this animal protein is not healthy. However, Americans seem to ignore all the research. Instead, they consume it morning, noon, and night, day after day.

What makes red meat so unhealthy? It is high in saturated fat, and from what you've learned so far, you know that is risky business.

If red meat is a staple in your diet, you are increasing your chances of cancer, high cholesterol, heart disease, hypertension, diabetes, and chronic inflammation.

Tips to Lose Weight Quickly

If you're ready to lose weight and get healthy, here are some tips on how to use the Mediterranean lifestyle to do just that.

Eat your biggest meal earlier

If you've been eating the standard American diet, you're probably used to eating your main meal when you're back home after a long day at the office. Traditionally, when eating the Mediterranean way, lunch is when you'll eat your main meal. When we hold out until later in the day, we end up extra hungry when it's time to eat dinner. This makes the risk of overeating so much higher.

Also, since one tends to be tired after work, the temptation may be to get some take-out instead of cooking food at home. I can almost guarantee that you'll end up eating more calories than you should. Not to mention the sodium and sugar overload that is part and parcel of fast food.

I was convinced of the pros of timing my food when I read a study declaring that out of two control groups, the group that consumed the bulk of their calories earlier during the day lost weight but the other group didn't (Garauletn et al. 2013). But what surprised me most was that both these groups ate precisely the same number of calories!

Continuing on the topic of eating, you have to eat more but also keep an eye on the size of your portions. I know, if that isn't a contradiction, I don't know what is. But let me explain.

Most vegetables are low-calorie yet very satiating. Since the Mediterranean Diet is centered around vegetables taking up the most space on your plate, you can end up eating too little at the end of the day. You may be asking yourself, Why is eating too little an issue? If limiting calories is what you need to do to lose weight, then the less you eat, the better. Not so? Unfortunately, if you cut your calories too much, it will lead to various health problems and can make you gain weight.

Each person has a set number of calories they need to eat per day. For example, generally, women between 19 and 30 years old who lead a sedentary lifestyle have a daily calorie requirement of 2000. Men of the same age and activity level need to eat 400 calories more, or 2400. That's just a benchmark, and you will have to take your current weight, height, and exercise habits into consideration.

For most people, eating less than 1200 calories per day will slow down their metabolism, and they will, over time, experience nutritional deficiencies. There's no way that you can meet your body's vitamin and mineral needs with food if you don't eat enough.

So, that is where the eat more part comes in – more veggies and other low-calorie plant-based foods that is. When it comes to portion control, it is the high-calorie foods like meat, grains, and fats that you want to keep your eyes on. Overeating these foods will make the dial on your calorie counter work overtime.

Vegetables are superfoods

I covered the benefits of filling your plate with a colorful assortment of plant-based foods. I cannot emphasize the importance of this enough. The high fiber content in vegetables will curb any cravings, and you won't experience that carb crash that typically happens after eating starchy sides.

Personally, I like cooking my vegetables in some olive oil and adding feta for some extra flavor.

Drink a lot of water

I'm sure you've seen this mentioned in countless weight-loss articles, and for a good reason. Water contains no calories. Drinking your calories is a big no-no. Take fruit juice, for example. It will make you feel full for a few minutes, but after that, you'll be hungry and will want to eat. You just wasted a amount of calories on something that basically just fell right through you. And the mind is a tricky thing. You can easily convince yourself that you haven't had any calories yet since it wasn't solid food. It's easy to overshoot your calorie target when that happens. Eat your fruit; don't drink it.

If you're bored with drinking water, coffee and tea (especially green tea) work well as substitutes within limits. It should never replace water entirely.

Control your cravings and quell your appetite

Luckily, the Mediterranean Diet is an appetite suppressant in disguise. You'll be eating a balanced diet of plant-based foods, good fats, and protein, which will make you feel satisfied. As an added bonus, most foods that form part of this diet have a low-glycemic index in comparison to the carb-heavy foods found in the standard American diet. Low-glycemic foods set off hormones that regulate your appetite and make you feel full.

When it comes to food cravings, I wish I could say you won't get them at all on the Mediterranean Diet. Although protein-rich foods and fat can help reduce your cravings, they won't eliminate them. Almost anything can trigger cravings, which are not only physiological in nature. If you had a bad day, you might experience a craving for chocolate as a means of psychological comfort.

The only tip I have is to prevent your blood sugar from spiking. Eat a snack every few hours to keep your glucose levels in check, and you'll be less likely to experience any overpowering cravings.

Get active and destress

Getting your heartbeat up when you're trying to lose weight is fundamental. It goes back to calories in versus calories out. If you exercise, you expend more energy, increasing your chances of reaching a calorie deficit. Not only that, your heart is a muscle, and exercise is a great way to strengthen your muscles!

When you're utilizing the Mediterranean Diet to lose weight, you have to get active for 30 minutes to an hour in the morning or evenings. It is best to get exercise throughout the day. Take a break from your desk and go for a walk. Do some stretches. Take the stairs and not the escalator. Anything that will get your heart beating a little faster is perfect.

One more benefit of regular exercise is stress reduction. The Mediterranean lifestyle supports leading a stress-free life, or rather a life as relaxed as possible in these times. By managing your stress, you will experience less anxiety over trivialities and enjoy life more. It will make all aspects of your life better, including your relationships with those around you. This is good because spending time with loved ones is a principle the Mediterranean lifestyle endorses.

Tips for Eating Out the Mediterranean Way

Sometimes being social creatures can make life extra hard, especially when you're trying to maintain a healthy lifestyle.

In the past, when I got invited out to dinner with friends or family, I immediately started to panic. That was before I learned to plot a course to the Mediterranean Basin on any menu! The fact that I was allowed to sip on a glass of red wine while planning my meal, of course, also helped to calm me down in the beginning.

Here are some quick tips you can use when dining out.

Remember the Basics

If you know what you can eat, you'll know what you can't eat. Keep the Mediterranean pyramid in mind when you're studying a menu. Select dishes that are plant-based, and instead of ordering a piece of steak, look for a fish or seafood option.

Go Vegetarian

If you don't see a fish, seafood, or poultry main dish that you want to sink your teeth into, choose a vegetarian option. Vegetarian meals usually contain plant-based protein and a grain, which means you get to eat a well-rounded meal.

Wine is the Drink of Choice

You're welcome to enjoy a glass of red wine with your food. Sip slowly and relish the taste. You're only allowed 4 oz. if you're a woman and 8 oz. if you're a man. It is up to you to make it last!

Divide Your Plate in Half

Unless you're eating at a French restaurant, you can bet on getting a portion big enough to feed two. I always end up taking half of the food on my plate home, which is perfect because then I don't have to worry about breakfast the next day.

The Oil Issue

Most restaurants don't use olive oil for cooking their foods. Sunflower oil is much cheaper. Avoid items on the menu that are oily. I suggest selecting grilled, baked, or roasted when given the option. But nothing is stopping you from getting your olive oil fill by adding some to your meal!

I hope that reduces some of the stress you were experiencing at the thought of eating at a restaurant. I have a feeling there's still some anxiety about what you should stock up on to transition to the Mediterranean Diet successfully.

Don't worry. I am ready to help you with a comprehensive shopping list you can take with you when heading to the grocery store.

Making time for yourself is self-care and highly recommended.

If you lead a highly stressful life, you may consider practicing deep breathing exercises or meditating to relax, but do take time out of your day for yourself. Make sure you get adequate sleep, eat healthily, and drink enough water to help bring those stress levels down.

It should now be apparent how interwoven the diet and lifestyle aspects are.

Chapter 2: Common Mistakes

When starting anything new, mistakes are unavoidable. In this chapter, I am going to give you a quick rundown of some of the mistakes I made when I first started eating the Mediterranean way, as well as share some slipups friends and family members had.

Mistake 1: Portion Control

I know I've been going on and on about moderation. I will, unfortunately, have to talk about it some more under the guise of portion control. Managing how much you eat is particularly important if you're trying to lose weight, but it is also a factor if you want to maintain your weight and, with it, your health.

It's not about controlling the number of vegetables you're eating. We've established that you will instinctively eat until you're full since veggies are high in fiber and, therefore, very filling.

You have to regulate everything else on your plate. Nuts and olive oil are the main culprits in eating too many calories without even realizing it. A recommended daily serving of nuts is one to two handfuls. Olive oil should be limited to two tablespoons per dish.

Mistake 2: Carb Overload

Although the Mediterranean Diet includes grains and cereals, including the oh-so-addicting bread and pasta varieties, it doesn't mean you should overeat. It is healthier to limit your carbohydrate intake, especially refined carbs, for all the reasons I mentioned earlier while discussing the Mediterranean food pyramid.

To motivate my reasoning even further, consider the fact that we are more sedentary than the people who traditionally worked the farms and went fishing. We drive and don't walk, and we take the escalator instead of using the stairs. The examples are endless.

This lower level of activity means we burn fewer calories than our ancestors, but we still want to eat more while doing less. No wonder so many people are overweight!

Mistake 3: Not Eating Enough Fish

You won't reap the heart- and brain-boosting health benefits of fish and seafood if you don't eat enough of it. Aim for three times a week, and you'll get all the omega-3 fatty acids your brain and body needs.

If you're a vegetarian or you dislike seafood, don't worry, just supplement with fish and seaweed oil.

Mistake 4: Eating the Wrong Dairy

Not all cheese is good for you. Pasteurized cheese, for example, isn't as nutrient-rich and doesn't contain as many probiotics as feta, mozzarella, Camembert. This also applies to yogurt. If you choose to buy those that are artificially flavored and packed full of sugar, you won't be doing your gut any favors. However, if you select plain Greek yogurt or, better yet, kefir, and flavor it yourself with fruit, nuts, and even some honey, your insides will do a happy dance.

Mistake 5: Banishing the Beans

Beans should be part of a healthy foundation of the Mediterranean meal plan. Some people prefer to leave this superfood off their plates because it takes longer to prepare than other food, and beans give some people gas. Considering that beans are oxidation fighters and helpful in regulating blood sugar, I suggest you put aside any objections you have against eating them.

Mistake 6: Thinking Wine is Water

It can be tempting to drink more wine than you're allowed. Yes, red wine does have health benefits as mentioned in the previous chapter. But it can't nor should it replace water.

First off, wine is not going to quench your thirst. It will actually make you thirstier. Also, the advantages of drinking water should not be overlooked. It's good for your kidneys and all other organs too, come to think of it. It helps your digestive system run smoothly. And my favorite perk from drinking enough water – soft, glowing skin.

Mistake 7: Using Extra-Virgin Olive Oil at a High Heat

When extra-virgin olive oil reaches 400 degrees Fahrenheit, it starts losing all the stuff that makes it good, as well as its flavor. Even more concerning, the oil will become pro-inflammatory due to the oxidation that takes place through heat damage. As you can see, overheating extra-virgin olive oil will not only damage your health but your pocketbook too. Who wants to eat olive oil with no taste?

Mistake 8: Not Obeying the 10 Commandments

It's not as serious as it sounds, I promise. But the 10 commandments perfectly sums up what the Mediterranean Diet and lifestyle is all about. And, if you follow them diligently, you're set to gain a healthy body and a longer life.

Don't worry if you wander off the path now and again. You won't be condemned to a sickly life spent in an out of shape body. Just get back to following the Mediterranean Diet and living the lifestyle, and you'll be a-okay.

The ten commandments of the Mediterranean Diet and lifestyle are:

1. Fill your plate with an abundance of fresh, non-processed food.
2. Do not let any saturated fat, trans fat, sodium, or refined sugar cross your lips.
3. Don't use margarine or butter; in its place use olive oil or trans-fat-free vegetable spread.
4. Eat your fill of vegetables but limit the portions of other foods.
5. Drink enough water.
6. Don't drink too much red wine.
7. Get your heart rate up for at least 30 minutes a day.
8. Don't smoke.
9. Unwind and relax, specifically after eating.
10. Laugh a lot, smile, and enjoy life.

Chapter 3 28-Day Meal Plan to Start with Mediterranean Diet

I have a confession to make; the fact that it is called the Mediterranean "Diet" annoys me. A diet is when you drastically cut your calories to the point of starvation. When you do eat, you force mostly dull and bland food down your throat and try to convince yourself it was delicious and enough. No wonder diets fail.

I would be happier if it were called the Mediterranean "Nutrition Plan," but regrettably, it is what it is. As long as you know that it's not a fad or a quick fix, I will push my discontent to the side.

I decided to include a 4-week example menu to help you find your feet. I realize starting down a new nutritional path can be confusing, but in this section, you will have a variety of meal ideas to choose from. Since you now know the fundamentals of the Mediterranean Diet, you may even feel ready to change things up and adapt the menu as you go along.

4 Weeks Meal Plan

	Breakfast	Lunch	Dinner
1	Roasted Grapes Yogurt Parfaits	Simple Confetti Couscous	Aromatic Whole Chicken
		Freekeh Pilaf With Walnuts And Sauce	Tabbouleh
2	Oats And Seeds Breakfast	Shrimp With Black Bean Pasta	Lentils And Bulgur Wheat And Browned Onions
		Portobello Caprese	Quick Sauteed Mushrooms
3	Baked Cherry And Almond Oatmeal Cups	Quick Spanish Rice	Caprese In Chicken
		Rosemary And Honey Almonds	Mushroom And Cheese Stuffed Tomatoes
4	Creamy Cherry And Pomegranate Smoothie	Creamy Polenta With Parmesan Cheese	Lemony Chicken Kebabs With Cherry Tomato Salad
		Za'Atar Flatbreads	Shakshuka
5	Chickpea Avocado Mash And Feta Toast	Simple Confetti Couscous	Spanish Flavor Braised Chicken Thighs With Almond Sauce
		Spinach Salad With Citrus Vinaigrette	Spicy Broccoli Rabe And Artichoke Hearts
6	Homemade Honey Nut Granola	Mediterranean Trout With Sautéed Vegetables	Lentils And Bulgur Wheat And Browned Onions
		Gemista	Shrimp Salad With Endive And Walnuts
7	Easy Scrambled Eggs With Sauteed Peppers	Quick Spanish Rice	Tagine
		Shredded Zucchini Salad	Spanakopita

	Breakfast	Lunch	Dinner
1	Buckwheat And Almond Milk Pancakes	Mediterranean Orzo And Vegetables Pilaf	Lemony Rosemary Chicken Thighs
		Easy Creamy Tzatziki Sauce	Citrus Pistachios And Asparagus
2	Brown Rice And Asparagus Tortilla Wraps	Chicken Breasts With Rustic Pesto	Rustic Lentil And Basmati Rice Pilaf
		Tomato And Parsley Stuffed Eggplant	Easy Lemon Garlic Hummus
3	Cucumber Sandwich With Hummus	Mediterranean Orzo And Vegetables Pilaf	Poached Salmon With Mustard Sauce
		Cantaloupe And Watermelon Caprese Salad	Quick Sauteed Mushrooms
4	Luscious Vegan Pita	Lemon-Herbs Orzo	Stuffed Squid With Spinach And Chees
		Simple Celery And Orange Salad	Ratatouille
5	Tomato Linguine	Browned Salmon Cakes	Mediterranean Sheet Pan Fish Fillets
		Gemista	Rosemary And Honey Almonds
6	Italian Flavor Ricotta And Tomato Pizza With Balsamic Glaze	Marinated Shrimp With Orange	Lemon-Herbs Orzo
		Brussels Sprouts With Balsamic Glaze	Feta Cheese And Olives Medley With Lemon Juice
7	Zucchini, Tomato, And Pine Nut Farfalle	Creamy Polenta With Parmesan Cheese	Rustic Lentil And Basmati Rice Pilaf
		Kale Salad With Pistachio And Parmesan	Stuffed Cabbage Rolls

	Breakfast	Lunch	Dinner
1	Spaghetti Al Limone	Rustic Lentil And Basmati Rice Pilaf	Red Wined Short Ribs
		Classic Tabouli Salad	Spinach Salad With Citrus Vinaigrette
2	Creamy Cherry And Pomegranate Smoothie	Simple Confetti Couscous	Grilled Halibut With Romesco Sauce
		Quick Sauteed Mushrooms	Rosemary And Honey Almonds
3	Chickpea Avocado Mash And Feta Toast	Quick Mussels With White Wine Sauce	Creamy Polenta With Parmesan Cheese
		Simple Celery And Orange Salad	Authentic Gazpacho Soup
4	Roasted Grapes Yogurt Parfaits	Lemon-Herbs Orzo	Quick Spanish Rice
		Shredded Zucchini Salad	Red Lentil Soup With Lemon
5	Homemade Honey Nut Granola	Greek Flavor Chicken With Salsa	Stuffed Squid With Spinach And Cheese
		Easy Lemon Garlic Hummus	Easy Vegetable And White Bean Soup
6	Oats And Seeds Breakfast	Mediterranean Orzo And Vegetables Pilaf	Lentils And Bulgur Wheat And Browned Onions
		Shakshuka	Za'Atar Flatbreads
7	Luscious Vegan Pita	Chicken In Greek Yogurt	Rustic Lentil And Basmati Rice Pilaf
		Portobello Caprese	Kale Salad With Pistachio And Parmesan

	Breakfast	Lunch	Dinner
1	Spaghetti Al Limone	Spanish Style Salmon With Vegetables	Quick Spanish Rice
		Mushroom And Cheese Stuffed Tomatoes	Freekeh Pilaf With Walnuts And Sauce
2	Brown Rice And Asparagus Tortilla Wraps	Rustic Lentil And Basmati Rice Pilaf	Lemony Chicken Kebabs With Cherry Tomato Salad
		Brussels Sprouts With Balsamic Glaze	Tomato And Parsley Stuffed Eggplant
3	Cucumber Sandwich With Hummus	Lemon-Herbs Orzo	Stuffed Squid With Spinach And Cheese
		Spicy Broccoli Rabe And Artichoke Hearts	Easy Lemon Garlic Hummus
4	Luscious Vegan Pita	Poached Salmon With Mustard Sauce	Simple Confetti Couscous
		Shredded Zucchini Salad	Citrus Pistachios And Asparagus
5	Homemade Honey Nut Granola	Browned Salmon Cakes	Chicken Breasts With Rustic Pesto
		Tagine	Gemista
6	Baked Cherry And Almond Oatmeal Cups	Aromatic Whole Chicken	Spanish Flavor Braised Chicken Thighs With Almond Sauce
		Stuffed Cabbage Rolls	Tabbouleh
7	Roasted Grapes Yogurt Parfaits	Mediterranean Orzo And Vegetables Pilaf	Mediterranean Trout With Sautéed Vegetables
		Ratatouille	Authentic Gazpacho Soup

Mediterranean Diet Shopping List

Before you go shopping, remember to look for fruits and veggies that are in season and easy to find where you live. There's no need for you to import something on this list if it's not readily available where you live.

Also, keep in mind that dairy products should be full-fat. Okay, grab the grocery cart and let's get to it!

Vegetables

- Tomatoes
- Onions
- Peppers
- Cucumbers
- Eggplant
- Zucchini
- Okra
- Green beans
- Potatoes
- Garlic
- Peas
- Mushrooms
- Broccoli
- Carrots
- Beets
- Cauliflower
- Celery
- Spinach
- Lettuce
- Cabbage
- You can also buy frozen spinach, green beans, and peas.

Fruits

- Apricots
- Avocado
- Oranges
- Lemons
- Apples
- Tangerines
- Pears
- Watermelon
- Cherries
- Peaches
- Cantaloupe
- Figs
- Strawberries
- Raspberries
- If there are other types of fruit local to your area, feel free to add to the list.

Meat and Poultry

- Chicken
- Ground beef
- Pork

Fish and Seafood

- Anchovies
- Sardines
- Salmon
- Shrimp
- Calamari
- Cod

Dairy

- Greek yogurt
- Feta cheese
- Other non-processed cheese
- Kefir

Grains and Bread	Herbs and Spices
◆ Whole grain bread ◆ Brown rice ◆ Bulgur ◆ Couscous ◆ Phyllo ◆ Pita bread	◆ Oregano ◆ Dill ◆ Parsley ◆ Cinnamon ◆ Mint ◆ All Spice ◆ Cumin ◆ Basil ◆ Pepper ◆ Salt
Fats and Nuts ◆ Olive oil ◆ Almonds ◆ Tahini ◆ Walnuts ◆ Pistachios ◆ Sesame seeds	**Pantry** ◆ Coffee ◆ Tea (Green and herbal) ◆ Canned tomatoes ◆ Olives ◆ Tomato paste ◆ Balsamic vinegar ◆ Honey ◆ Sun dried tomatoes ◆ Capers
Beans ◆ White beans ◆ Lentils ◆ Fava beans ◆ Chickpeas	
Greens ◆ Beet greens ◆ Chicory ◆ Amaranth ◆ Dandelion	

There you go, an uncomplicated shopping list you can use to buy everything you need to move from the standard American diet to the Mediterranean Diet.

In the remaining chapters of this book, I will share with you some of my favorite Mediterranean recipes.

You can expect everyday recipes you can make for your family but also something for those special occasions when you want to show off your culinary skills. Is there a better way to impress your guests than with a lively plate filled with multicolored vegetables and tender fish given a golden glow by the olive oil you sautéed it in? Oh, and don't forget a glass of red wine, perfectly paired with the dish. I suggest Pinot Noir with any fish dish.

Don't forget to toast to a good life and even better health!

Chapter 4 Breakfast

OATS AND SEEDS BREAKFAST

Prep time: 10 minutes | Cook time: 0 minutes | Serves 2

¼ cup pistachios, shelled
½ cup gluten-free old-fashioned oats
2 tablespoons chia seeds
3 tablespoons pumpkin seeds
½ cup plain Greek yogurt
¾ cup unsweetened almond milk
2 to 3 teaspoons maple syrup
½ cup pomegranate arils

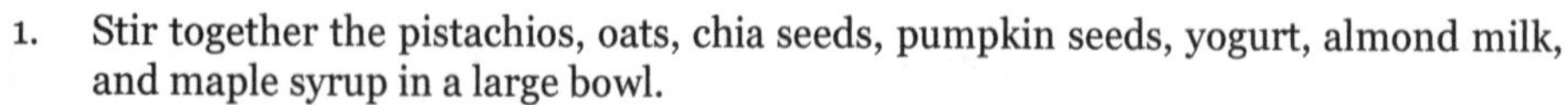

1. Stir together the pistachios, oats, chia seeds, pumpkin seeds, yogurt, almond milk, and maple syrup in a large bowl.
2. Evenly divide the mixture into two mason jars and scatter the tops with pomegranate arils.
3. Cover the mason jars and refrigerate to chill for at least 3 hours, preferably overnight.
4. Remove from the refrigerator and serve chilled.

TIP: Fresh or frozen berries can be substituted for the pomegranates. Besides, thick-cut oats can provide an excellent and hearty texture.

PER SERVING:
Calories: 504 | total fat: 24.1g | total carbs: 60.2g | fiber: 9.7g | sugar: 32g | protein: 16.5g | sodium: 172mg | cholesterol: 21mg

CHICKPEA AVOCADO MASH AND FETA TOAST

Prep time: 10 minutes | Cook time: 0 minutes| Serves 4

1 (15-ounce / 425-g) can chickpeas, drained and rinsed
1 avocado, pitted
2 teaspoons freshly squeezed lemon juice or 1 tablespoon orange juice
½ cup feta cheese, diced
½ teaspoon freshly ground black pepper
4 pieces multigrain toast
2 teaspoons honey

SPECIAL EQUIPMENT:
A potato masher

1. In a large bowl, add the chickpeas. Using a large spoon, scoop the avocado flesh out of the skin and transfer to the bowl of chickpeas.
2. Mash them with a potato masher or the back of a fork, until a uniform consistency is achieved. Fold in the lemon juice, diced feta cheese, and black pepper. Stir to combine well.
3. Divide the mashed chickpeas mixture onto each piece of multigrain toast, spreading it all over.
4. To serve, drizzle the toasts with honey.

TIP: If the low-sodium canned chickpeas are not available, you can reduce the sodium content by as much as 40% via draining and rinsing the canned beans.

PER SERVING:
Calories: 346 | total fat: 23.3g | saturated fat: 6.2g | total carbs: 27.1g | fiber: 11.2g | protein: 12.2g | sugar: 7.1g | sodium: 318mg | phosphorus: 296mg | potassium: 415mg | cholesterol: 18mg

HOMEMADE HONEY NUT GRANOLA

Prep time: 10 minutes | Cook time: 20 minutes| Serves 6

2½ cups regular rolled oats
⅓ cup almonds, coarsely chopped
½ teaspoon ground cinnamon
⅛ teaspoon sea salt
¼ cup olive oil
2 tablespoons ground flaxseed
½ cup chopped dried apricots
¼ cup honey
2 teaspoons vanilla extract

1. Preheat the oven to 325°F (160°C). Line a rimmed baking sheet with parchment paper and set aside.
2. Heat a large nonstick skillet over medium-high heat. Add the oats, almonds, cinnamon, and salt, cook for about 6 minutes, stirring frequently.
3. Meanwhile, mix together the olive oil, flaxseed, apricots, and honey in a microwave-safe bowl and microwave on high for 1 minute, or until bubbles form. When cooled slightly, add the vanilla and stir well. Pour it into the skillet of oat mixture.
4. Stir the oat mixture one more time, then transfer to the prepared baking sheet.
5. Bake in the preheated oven until lightly browned, about 15 minutes.
6. Remove from the oven to a wire rack to cool completely before slicing into small pieces.

TIP: You can heat the mixture of Step 3 in a saucepan over medium heat for 3 to 4 minutes. The nut granola tastes great paired with a dollop of plain Greek yogurt.

PER SERVING:
Calories: 257 | total fat: 8.2g | saturated fat: 1.2g | total carbs: 42.3g | fiber: 6.3g | protein: 6.1g | sugar: 18.2g | sodium: 138mg | phosphorus: 175mg | potassium: 293mg | cholesterol: 4mg

TIP: Remember to cook the eggs over low heat for preventing tough scrambled eggs.

PER SERVING:
Calories: 261 | total fat: 16.3g | saturated fat: 5.1g | total carbs: 2.2g | fiber: 1.1g | protein: 29.2g | sugar: 1.1g | sodium: 178mg | phosphorus: 385mg | potassium: 350mg |cholesterol: 355mg

EASY SCRAMBLED EGGS WITH SAUTEED PEPPERS

Prep time: 5 minutes | Cook time: 10 minutes| Serves 4

6 large eggs
2 tablespoons water
¼ teaspoon sea salt
1½ teaspoons extra-virgin olive oil
1 cup bell peppers, chopped
2 garlic cloves, minced
½ cup goat cheese, crumbled
2 tablespoons chopped fresh mint

1. Whisk together the eggs, water, and salt in a medium bowl until frothy. Set aside.
2. In a large skillet, heat the olive oil over medium-high heat.
3. Sauté the bell peppers for about 5 minutes until wilted, stirring occasionally.
4. Toss in the garlic cloves and cook for 1 minute until fragrant.
5. Reduce the heat to medium-low and pour the whisked eggs over the top of bell peppers in the skillet. Let it cook undisturbed for about 2 minutes, or until the eggs are beginning to set around the edges. Add the goat cheese and continue to scramble until the eggs are soft and the cheese melts, about 1 to 2 minutes.
6. Remove from the heat to a plate. Sprinkle the chopped mint on top for garnish before serving.

BUCKWHEAT AND ALMOND MILK PANCAKES

Prep time: 15 minutes | Cook time: 5 minutes | Serves 2

DRY INGREDIENTS:
½ teaspoon cardamom
½ cup buckwheat flour
½ teaspoon baking powder
¼ teaspoon baking soda

WET INGREDIENTS:
1 egg, beaten
¼ cup plain Greek yogurt
½ cup unsweetened almond milk
1 tablespoon maple syrup
½ teaspoon orange extract

1. Mix together the cardamom, buckwheat flour, baking powder, and baking soda in a large bowl.
2. In a separate bowl, combine the beaten egg, yogurt, almond milk, maple syrup, and orange extract, whisking thoroughly.
3. Pour the wet ingredients into the bowl of dry ingredients. Stir well with a fork until you get a smooth batter.
4. Heat a large skillet over high heat until hot.
5. Reduce the heat to medium, then slowly pour the batter into the pan, tilting the pan to spread evenly. Cook for about 2 to 3 minutes until golden. Carefully flip it over and cook for 1 minute more.
6. Remove from the heat and serve on plates.

TIP: If you don't have a large skillet that fits all the batter, you can cook the pancakes in batches. To add more flavors to this meal, you can serve it with a drizzle of maple syrup or some fresh berries.

PER SERVING:
Calories: 198 | total fat: 6.3g | total carbs: 27.2g | fiber: 3.2g | sugar: 6.1g | protein: 10.1g | sodium: 243mg | cholesterol: 95mg

BAKED CHERRY AND ALMOND OATMEAL CUPS

Prep time: 10 minutes | Cook time: 20 to 30 minutes | Serves 4

1 tablespoon olive oil
1 cup gluten-free old-fashioned oats
4 tablespoons almonds, sliced
4 tablespoons maple syrup
¾ cup unsweetened almond milk
2 cup chopped cherries
2 egg, beaten
1 teaspoon almond extract
1 teaspoon vanilla
Pinch salt
Plain Greek yogurt (optional)
Ricotta cheese crumbles (optional)

SPECIAL EQUIPMENT:
A 4-cup muffin tin

1. Preheat the oven to 350°F (180°C). Lightly grease 4 muffin tin cups with olive oil and set aside.
2. Combine all ingredients in a large bowl and stir until completely mixed.
3. Spoon the mixture into the greased muffins cups, filling each about three-quarters full.
4. Bake in the preheated oven for about 20 to 30 minutes, or until the tops spring back lightly when gently pressed with your fingertip.
5. Allow to cool for about 10 minutes. Serve it with a drizzle of plain Greek yogurt or a sprinkle of cheese, if desired.

TIP: You can store the leftovers in the fridge for several days. If you cannot find the fresh berries, frozen berries will work, too.

PER SERVING:
Calories: 290 | total fat: 9.2g | total carbs: 43.1g | fiber: 4.1g | sugar: 23.9g | protein: 10.7g | sodium: 156mg | cholesterol: 90mg

CREAMY CHERRY AND POMEGRANATE SMOOTHIE

Prep time: 5 minutes | Cook time: 0 minutes| Serves 4

16 ounces (454 g) dark sweet cherries
1½ cups plain Greek yogurt, plus more if needed
⅓ cup unsweetened almond milk, plus more if needed
¾ cup pomegranate juice
¾ teaspoon ground cinnamon
1 teaspoon vanilla extract
6 ice cubes
½ cup fresh pomegranate seeds
½ cup chopped pistachios

1. Put the cherries, yogurt, almond milk, pomegranate juice, cinnamon, vanilla extract, and ice cubes in a blender. Blend until uniform and smooth.
2. Pour into four smoothie glasses, and sprinkle the tops evenly with pomegranate seeds and pistachios. Serve chilled or at room temperature.

TIP: You can add a few tablespoons of plain Greek yogurt, if your smoothie gets too thin. Instead, try add a few tablespoons of unsweetened almond milk to loosen it up if thick.

PER SERVING:
Calories: 278 | total fat: 10.4g | saturated fat: 2.1g | total carbs: 41.3g | fiber: 27.1g | protein: 5.4g | sugar: 31.8g | sodium: 49.1mg | phosphorus: 149.2mg | potassium: 641mg | cholesterol: 6mg

ROASTED GRAPES YOGURT PARFAITS

Prep time: 5 minutes | Cook time: 20 minutes| Serves 4

1½ pounds (680 g) seedless grapes, stems removed
1 tablespoon olive oil
2 cups plain Greek yogurt
½ cup walnuts, chopped
4 teaspoons honey

1. Put a rimmed baking sheet in an oven and preheat the oven to 450°F (235°C).
2. Rinse the grapes and dry thoroughly with paper towels, then transfer to a bowl. Add the olive oil and toss well until coated fully.
3. Using potholders, carefully remove the hot baking sheet from the oven, and transfer the oiled grapes to the baking sheet.
4. Roast in the preheated oven for about 20 minutes, shaking the pan occasionally, or until the grapes are beginning to shrunk.
5. Remove from the oven to a wire rack to rest for 5 minutes until slightly cooled.
6. Meanwhile, divide the yogurt among four tall parfait glasses. Top each glass evenly with chopped walnut and honey.
7. Scatter each parfait with the cooled grapes before serving.

TIP: You can reserve the grape stems. Arrange the grapes on the baking sheet and brush them with olive oil. Remove the stems from the grapes before serving.

PER SERVING
Calories: 295 | total fat: 12.3g | saturated fat: 4.1g | total carbs: 43.2g | fiber: 2.1g | protein: 7.1g | sugar: 38.2g | sodium: 91mg | phosphorus: 187mg | potassium: 563mg | cholesterol: 18mg

Chapter 5 Small Plates And Snacks

ROSEMARY AND HONEY ALMONDS

Prep time: 5 minutes | Cook time: 5 minutes | Serves 6

1 cup raw, whole, shelled almonds
1 tablespoon minced fresh rosemary
¼ teaspoon sea salt
1 tablespoon honey
Nonstick cooking spray

1. Add the almonds, rosemary, and salt to a large skillet over medium heat, stirring for 1 minute.
2. Add the honey and cook for an additional 3 to 4 minutes, stirring frequently, or until the almonds are evenly coated and beginning to become darken.
3. Remove from the heat to a large plate. Spray the almonds with nonstick cooking spray, then let them cool for at least 10 minutes.
4. If the almonds stick together, just break apart before serving.

TIP: You can try this recipe with your favorites nuts, such as pecans or walnuts. If you're not keen on the honey, maple syrup will work, too.

PER SERVING:
Calories: 13 | total fat: 1.1g | saturated fat: 0g | total carbs: 3.1g | fiber: 1.1g | protein: 1.2g | sugar: 3.2g | sodium: 96mg | phosphorus: 2mg | potassium: 4mg | cholesterol: 0mg

OLIVES MEDLEY WITH LEMON JUICE

Prep time: 10 minutes | Cook time: 0 minutes | Serves 8

1 (1-pound / 454-g) block of Greek feta cheese
3 cups mixed olives (Kalamata and green), drained from brine; pitted preferred

DRESSING:
¼ cup extra-virgin olive oil
1 teaspoon grated lemon zest
3 tablespoons lemon juice
1 teaspoon dried oregano

Pita bread, for serving

1. On a flat work surface, slice the Greek feta cheese into squares about ½ inch, then transfer to a large bowl.
2. Add the olives to the bowl of feta cheese and mix well. Set aside.
3. Make the dressing: Stir together the olive oil, lemon zest, lemon juice, and oregano in a separate bowl until well combined.
4. Drizzle the feta cheese and olives with the dressing, then toss gently until coated fully.
5. Serve the feta cheese and olives alongside the pita bread.

TIP: For extra kick, you can try add ½ teaspoon red pepper flakes to this dressing.

PER SERVING:
Calories: 408 | total fat: 38.3g | saturated fat: 12.2g | total carbs: 8.3g | fiber: 0g | protein: 8.4g | sugar: 2g | cholesterol: 54 mg

QUICK SAUTEED MUSHROOMS

Prep time: 10 minutes | Cook time: 10 minutes | Serves 4 to 6

3 tablespoons olive oil
2 tablespoons garlic, minced
2 pounds (907 g) cremini mushrooms, halved
½ teaspoon salt
½ teaspoon freshly ground black pepper

1. Heat the olive oil in a skillet over medium heat.
2. Sauté the minced garlic in the olive oil for 2 minutes until fragrant, stirring occasionally.
3. Add the halved mushrooms and stir to combine. Sauté for about 8 minutes, stirring frequently, or until the mushrooms are tender.
4. Remove from the heat to a plate. To serve, sprinkle the sautéed mushrooms with black pepper.

TIP: To add more flavors to this meal, serve it topped with freshly chopped chives or parsley. It can be served as a topping for pizza, pasta, or potatoes.

PER SERVING:
Calories: 185 | total fat: 9.3g | saturated fat: 5.2g | total carbs: 10.1g | fiber: 3.2g | protein: 9.2g | sugar: 3g | sodium: 335mg | cholesterol: 23.1mg

FREEKEH PILAF WITH WALNUTS AND SAUCE

Prep time: 15 minutes | Cook time: 20 minutes | Serves 4

FREEKEH PILAF:
2½ cups freekeh
3 tablespoons olive oil, divided
2 medium diced onions
¼ teaspoon ground allspice
¼ teaspoon ground cinnamon
½ cup chopped walnuts
5 cups chicken stock
Salt and freshly ground black pepper, to taste

SAUCE:
½ cup plain Greek yogurt
1½ teaspoons freshly squeezed lemon juice
½ teaspoon garlic powder
Salt, to taste

1. Soak the freekeh in a bowl filled with cold water for about 5 minutes. Drain the freekeh in a sieve and rinse well under cold running water.
2. Heat 2 tablespoons olive oil in a skillet over medium heat. Sauté the onions for about 2 minutes until translucent. Add the freekeh, allspice, and cinnamon, stirring for 1 minute.
3. Pour in the walnuts and chicken broth, then season with salt and pepper. Bring them to a simmer for 2 minutes. Reduce the heat to low and cook covered for about 15 minutes until the freekeh is tender.
4. Remove from the heat and let it rest for 5 minutes until cooled slightly.
5. Meanwhile, mix together the yogurt, lemon juice, and garlic powder in a bowl. Season as needed with salt.
6. Serve the freekeh with the yogurt sauce on the side.

TIP: Adding the dried cranberries to this recipe can bring the dish a sweet crunchiness.

PER SERVING:
Calories: 657 | total fat: 25.3g | saturated fat: 3.2g | total carbs: 91.3g | fiber: 12.3g | protein: 23.3g | sugar: 4.2g | sodium: 578mg | cholesterol:6 mg

EASY LEMON GARLIC HUMMUS

Prep time: 5 minutes | Cook time: 0 minutes | Serves 6

1 (15-ounce / 425-g) can chickpeas, drained and liquid reserved
2 tablespoons peanut butter
3 tablespoons freshly squeezed lemon juice
2 garlic cloves
3 tablespoons extra-virgin olive oil, divided
¼ teaspoon sea salt
Raw veggies, for serving (optional)

1. Put the chickpeas and reserved liquid in a food processor, along with the peanut butter, lemon juice, garlic cloves, and 2 tablespoons of olive oil. Process the ingredients into a smooth hummus, about 1 to 2 minutes.
2. Transfer the hummus to a bowl. Drizzle with the remaining olive oil and season with ¼ teaspoon sea salt.
3. Serve it with raw veggies, if desired.

TIP: The hummus also can be served as a dip for whole-grain crackers. You can try add some spices of your choice to create your own recipe.

PER SERVING:
Calories: 127 | total fat: 6.1g | saturated fat: 1.2g | total carbs: 14.2g | fiber: 3.2g | protein: 4.2g | sugar: 3.1g | sodium: 367mg | phosphorus: 56mg | potassium: 83mg | cholesterol: 4mg

ZA'ATAR FLATBREADS

Prep time: 5 minutes | Cook time: 12 minutes | Serves 6

1 (16-ounce / 454-g) bag whole-wheat pizza dough
3 tablespoons olive oil
3 tablespoons sesame seeds
3 tablespoons dried thyme
¼ teaspoon kosher or sea salt
Nonstick cooking spray

1. Preheat the oven to 450°F (235°C) and coat a large baking sheet with nonstick cooking spray. Set aside.
2. Make the flatbreads: On a lightly floured surface, divide the pizza dough into three uniform balls. Using a rolling pin to roll them into 6-inch dough circles, then arrange on the prepared baking sheet.
3. Mix the olive oil, sesame seeds, thyme, and salt together in a bowl. Stir to incorporate. Brush each dough circle generously with the olive oil mixture with a pastry brush or spoon.
4. Bake in the preheated oven for 10 to 12 minutes until the dough circles turn golden brown around the edges and puff slightly.
5. Remove the flatbreads from the oven. Allow to cool for 5 minutes before cutting them in half.

TIP: To save time, you can use whole-wheat pita bread or lavash bread and a packaged za'atar spice blend.

PER SERVING:
Calories: 67 | total fat: 6.2g | saturated fat: 1.1g | total carbs: 3.2g | fiber: 1.2g | protein: 2.2g | sugar: 0g | sodium: 181mg | phosphorus: 36mg | potassium: 31mg | cholesterol: 3mg

EASY CREAMY TZATZIKI SAUCE

Prep time: 10 minutes | Cook time: 0 minutes | Serves 6

2 Persian cucumbers
3 cups plain Greek yogurt
2 medium minced garlic cloves
1 teaspoon dried dill
½ teaspoon salt

1. Rinse the cucumbers and cut off both tips. Peel the skin from the cucumbers with a vegetable peeler and dice them on your cutting board.
2. Transfer the diced cucumbers to a large bowl, and add the yogurt, minced garlic, dill, and salt. Stir well with a fork until completely blended.
3. Cover with plastic wrap and put it in the fridge to let the cucumbers marinate in the sauce for a few hours. Serve chilled.

TIP: Slicing off both ends of cucumbers can get rid of this bitterness. For added color and twist, serve drizzled with some olive oil.

PER SERVING:
Calories: 132 | total fat: 6.3g | saturated fat: 3.2g | total carbs: 7.3g | fiber: 1.2g | protein: 11.3g | sugar: 5.2g | sodium: 238mg | cholesterol: 18mg

Chapter 6 Salads And Soups

SPINACH SALAD WITH CITRUS VINAIGRETTE

Prep time: 10 minutes | Cook time: 0 minutes | Serves 4

CITRUS VINAIGRETTE:
¼ cup extra-virgin olive oil
3 tablespoons balsamic vinegar
½ teaspoon fresh lemon zest
½ teaspoon salt

SALAD:
1 pound (454 g) baby spinach, washed, stems removed
1 large ripe tomato, cut into ¼-inch pieces
1 medium red onion, thinly sliced

1. Make the citrus vinaigrette: Stir together the olive oil, balsamic vinegar, lemon zest, and salt in a bowl until mixed well.
2. Make the salad: Place the baby spinach, tomato and onions in a separate salad bowl. Pour the citrus vinaigrette over the salad and gently toss until the vegetables are coated thoroughly.

TIP: You can top the salad with some toasted pine nuts for additional crunch. And the baby spinach can be replaced with other leafy greens of your choice.

PER SERVING:
Calories: 173 | total fat: 14.2g | saturated fat: 2.2g | total carbs: 10.2g | fiber: 4.2g | protein: 4.1g | sugar: 2.2g | sodium: 388mg | cholesterol: 0mg

SIMPLE CELERY AND ORANGE SALAD

Prep time: 15 minutes | Cook time: 0 minutes | Serves 6

SALAD:
3 celery stalks, including leaves, sliced diagonally into ½-inch slices
½ cup green olives
¼ cup sliced red onion
2 large peeled oranges, cut into rounds

DRESSING:
1 tablespoon extra-virgin olive oil
1 tablespoon freshly squeezed lemon or orange juice
1 tablespoon olive brine
¼ teaspoon kosher or sea salt
¼ teaspoon freshly ground black pepper

1. Make the salad: Put the celery stalks, green olives, onion, and oranges in a shallow bowl. Mix well and set aside.
2. Make the dressing: In a separate bowl, combine the olive oil, lemon juice, olive brine, salt, and pepper. Stir with a fork to combine well.
3. Pour the dressing into the bowl of salad and lightly toss until coated thoroughly.
4. Serve chilled or at room temperature.

TIP: If you like the tart and sweet flavor, you can use the mandarin oranges instead of the oranges in this recipe.

PER SERVING:
Calories: 24 | total fat: 1.2g | saturated fat: 0g | total carbs: 2.2g | fiber: 1.2g | protein: 1.1g | sugar: 2.3g | sodium: 135mg | phosphorus: 5mg | potassium: 52mg | cholesterol: 2mg

CANTALOUPE AND WATERMELON CAPRESE SALAD

Prep time: 20 minutes | Cook time: 0 minutes | Serves 6

1 cantaloupe, quartered and seeded
½ small seedless watermelon
1 cup grape tomatoes
2 tablespoons extra-virgin olive oil
1 tablespoon balsamic vinegar
2 cups (about 8 ounces) fresh Mozzarella balls
⅓ cup fresh basil, torn into small pieces
¼ teaspoon kosher or sea salt
¼ teaspoon freshly ground black pepper

1. On your cutting board, slice the cantaloupe and watermelon into bite-sized pieces. Transfer them to a colander over a large bowl.
2. Drain and reserve the juice from the large bowl in a seal airtight container. Place the juice in the fridge to chill for later use.
3. In a separate bowl, add the cantaloupe, watermelon, tomatoes, olive oil, vinegar, Mozzarella balls, basil, salt, and pepper. Lightly toss them until well blended.
4. Serve the salad with the reserved juice on the side.

TIP: This salad perfectly goes well with avocado toast or cheese sandwiches.

PER SERVING:
Calories: 59 | total fat: 2.1g | saturated fat: 1.1g | total carbs: 9.2g | fiber: 1.2g | protein:1.1 g | sugar: 5.2g | sodium: 157mg | phosphorus: 13mg | potassium: 220mg | cholesterol: 3mg

SHRIMP SALAD WITH ENDIVE AND WALNUTS

Prep time: 10 minutes | Cook time: 2 minutes | Serves 4

VINAIGRETTE:
¼ cup olive oil
1 tablespoon Dijon mustard
1 small minced shallot
Juice and zest of 1 lemon
Sea salt and freshly ground black pepper, to taste

SALAD:
14 shrimp, peeled and deveined
2 cups salted water
1 head endive, broken into pieces
½ cup tart green apple, diced
2 tablespoons toasted walnuts

1. Make the vinaigrette: In a small bowl, whisk together the olive oil, Dijon mustard, shallot, lemon juice and zest, salt, and pepper until blended.
2. Cover the bowl with plastic wrap and refrigerate to chill until ready to use.
3. Put the shrimp into a saucepan of boiling salted water and cook for about 2 minutes, or until the shrimp is opaque.
4. Remove from the heat, drain and cool the shrimp under running cold water.
5. Make the salad: Spread out the endive pieces on a plate and scatter the top with the shrimp, diced apple, and toasted walnuts.
6. To serve, drizzle the salad evenly with the prepared vinaigrette.

TIP: To make this a complete meal, you can serve it with crusty bread and a dry white wine on the side.

PER SERVING:
Calories: 305 | total fat: 16.4g | total carbs: 7.8g | fiber: 4.8g | protein: 5g | sugar: 2g | sodium: 186mg | phosphorus: 84mg | potassium: 470mg | cholesterol: 28mg

SHREDDED ZUCCHINI SALAD

Prep time: 10 minutes | Cook time: 0 minutes | Serves 2

1 medium zucchini, shredded or sliced paper thin
6 halved cherry tomatoes
3 tablespoons olive oil
Juice of 1 lemon
Sea salt and freshly ground black pepper, to taste
3 to 4 basil leaves, thinly sliced
2 tablespoons Parmesan cheese, grated

1. Divide the zucchini slices between two serving plates. Spread the halved tomatoes on top.
2. Drizzle each plate evenly with the olive oil and lemon juice, then sprinkle with salt and pepper.
3. Serve topped with basil leaves and Parmesan cheese.

TIP: The zucchini needs to be thinly sliced. To save time, you can use a cheese grater or mandoline to shred the zucchini quickly and uniformly.

PER SERVING:
Calories: 55 | total fat: 21g | saturated fat: 3.5g | total carbs: 2.5g | fiber: 0.1g | protein: 1.7g | sugar: 0.6g | sodium: 91mg | phosphorus: 38mg | potassium: 59mg | cholesterol: 4mg

CLASSIC TABOULI SALAD

Prep time: 30 minutes | Cook time: 0 minutes | Serves 8 to 10

SALAD:
1 cup ground bulgur wheat, rinsed and drained
2 cups ripe tomato, finely diced
1 cup green onion, finely chopped
4 cups Italian parsley, finely chopped

DRESSING:
½ cup extra-virgin olive oil
½ cup lemon juice
1 teaspoon dried mint
1½ teaspoons salt

1. Make the salad: In a large bowl, add the bulgur wheat, tomatoes, green onion, and parsley. Set aside.
2. Make the dressing: In a separate bowl, mix together the olive oil, lemon juice, mint, and salt.
3. Pour the dressing into the bowl of salad and gently toss until coated well.
4. Serve chilled or at room temperature.

TIP: For extra kick, you can try add ¼ teaspoon cayenne pepper to this salad.

PER SERVING:
Calories: 209 | total fat: 4.2g | saturated fat: 2.1g | total carbs: 20.1g | fiber: 5.3g | protein: 4.2g | sugar: 1.1g | sodium: 460mg | cholesterol: 0mg

AUTHENTIC GAZPACHO SOUP

Prep time: 15 minutes | Cook time: 0 minutes | Serves 6 to 8

½ cup of water
2 slices of whole-grain bread, crust removed
1 Persian cucumber, peeled and chopped
2 pounds (907 g) ripe tomatoes
1 clove garlic, finely chopped
⅓ cup extra-virgin olive oil, plus more for serving
2 tablespoons red wine vinegar
1 teaspoon salt
½ teaspoon freshly ground black pepper

1. Soak the bread in a bowl of water for about 5 minutes, then discard the water.
2. In a food processor, put the bread, cucumber, tomatoes, garlic, olive oil, red wine vinegar, salt, and pepper. Process the ingredients until completely mixed and glossy.
3. Pour the mixture into a glass jar and refrigerate to chill until ready to serve.
4. To serve, drizzle the soup with olive oil.

TIP: To add more flavors to this meal, you can top the soup with fresh herbs of your choice, such as thyme, basil or parsley. For added crispness and sweetness, you can add ½ red onion.

PER SERVING:
Calories: 165 | total fat: 13.3g | saturated fat: 2.1g | total carbs: 12.2g | fiber: 2.1g | protein: 2.2g | sugar: 1.1g | sodium: 440mg | cholesterol: 0mg

EASY VEGETABLE AND WHITE BEAN SOUP

Prep time: 10 minutes | Cook time: 25 minutes | Serves 6

3 tablespoons extra-virgin olive oil
3 large garlic cloves, minced
1 large onion, finely chopped
2 cups celery, diced
2 cups carrots, diced
2 (15-ounce / 425-g) cans white beans, rinsed and drained
8 cups vegetable broth
1 teaspoon salt
½ teaspoon freshly ground black pepper

1. Heat the olive oil in a saucepan over medium heat. Cook the garlic and onion for about 3 minutes until golden brown.
2. Toss in the celery and carrots and sauté for about 4 minutes more until the vegetables are tender but still crisp, stirring occasionally.
3. Add the white beans and vegetable broth while whisking. Season with salt and pepper. Give it a good stir and bring to a simmer for 16 minutes, stirring occasionally, or until the soup is smooth and thickened.
4. Remove from the heat and serve while warm.

TIP: To add more flavors to this soup, you can add the chopped Swiss chard during the cooking. And serve topped with grated Parmesan cheese.

PER SERVING:
Calories: 247 | total fat: 7.3g | saturated fat: 1.3g | total carbs: 36.2g | fiber: 10.2g | protein: 9.2g | sugar: 8.1g | sodium: 503mg | cholesterol: 2mg

RED LENTIL SOUP WITH LEMON

Prep time: 10 minutes | Cook time: 50 minutes | Serves 6 to 8

1 cup red lentils, picked over and rinsed
½ cup long grain or basmati rice, rinsed
10 cups water
2 teaspoons salt
3 tablespoons extra-virgin olive oil
1 large finely chopped onion
2 cups finely diced carrots
1 teaspoon turmeric
1 lemon, cut into wedges

1. Add the red lentils, rice, water and salt to a large saucepan over medium heat. Allow to simmer covered for about 30 minutes, or until the lentils are soft, stirring occasionally.
2. Meanwhile, heat the olive oil in a skillet over medium-low heat until shimmering. Add the onions and sauté for 5 minutes until the edges are browned.
3. Put the onions, carrots, and turmeric into the soup in the saucepan and cook for 15 minutes more, whisking occasionally, or until the carrots are tender.
4. Divide the soup into serving bowls and serve drizzled with lemon juice squeezed from the wedges.

TIP: The soup can be made ahead, but don't add the lemon juice from the wedges before serving. For added color and flavor, garnish it with the chopped parsley.

PER SERVING:
Calories: 235 | total fat: 8.3g | saturated fat:1.2 g | total carbs: 8.2g | fiber: 9.1g | protein: 9.2g | sugar: 3.2g | sodium: 805mg | cholesterol: 0mg

KALE SALAD WITH PISTACHIO AND PARMESAN

Prep time: 20 minutes | Cook time: 0 minutes | Serves 6

6 cups raw kale, stemmed and chopped
¼ cup extra-virgin olive oil
2 tablespoons freshly squeezed lemon juice
½ teaspoon smoked paprika
2 cups chopped arugula
⅓ cup unsalted pistachios, shelled
6 tablespoons Parmesan cheese, shredded

1. Put the kale, olive oil, lemon juice, and paprika in a large bowl. Using your hands to massage the sauce into the kale until coated completely. Allow the kale to marinate for about 10 minutes.
2. When ready to serve, add the arugula and pistachios into the bowl of kale. Toss well and divide the salad into six salad bowls. Serve sprinkled with 1 tablespoon shredded Parmesan cheese.

TIP: Massaging the fresh trimmed kale or arugula with olive oil can tenderize them, which can be a delicious base for the salad.

PER SERVING:
Calories: 106 | total fat: 9.2g | saturated fat: 2.1g | total carbs: 4.2g | fiber: 2.1g | protein: 4.2g | sugar:1.2 g | sodium: 175mg | phosphorus: 83mg | potassium: 190mg | cholesterol: 6mg

Chapter 7 Beans, Rice, And Grains

SIMPLE CONFETTI COUSCOUS

Prep time: 5 minutes | Cook time: 20 minutes | Serves 4 to 6

3 tablespoons olive oil
1 large chopped onion
1 cup fresh peas
2 carrots, chopped
½ cup golden raisins
1 teaspoon salt
2 cups vegetable broth
2 cups couscous

1. Add the olive oil, onions, peas, raisins, and carrots to a skillet over medium heat. Allow to cook for 5 minutes, stirring occasionally, or until the vegetables start to soften.
2. Season with salt and pour in the vegetable broth while whisking. Bring it to a boil for about 5 minutes.
3. Fold in the couscous and stir to combine. Reduce the heat to low and cook covered for about 10 minutes, or until the couscous has absorbed the liquid completely.
4. Using a fork to fluff the couscous and serve while warm.

TIP: You can try any of your favorite vegetables besides the carrots and peas. To add more flavors to this meal, serve it with freshly chopped parsley or Parmesan cheese.

PER SERVING:
Calories: 515 | total fat: 12.3g | saturated fat: 2.2g | total carbs: 92.3g | fiber: 7.2g | protein: 14.2g | sugar: 17.1g | sodium: 505mg | cholesterol: 0mg

MEDITERRANEAN ORZO AND VEGETABLES PILAF

Prep time: 20 minutes | Cook time: 10 minutes | Serves 6

2 cups orzo
1 cup Kalamata olives
1 pint (2 cups) cherry tomatoes, cut in half
½ cup fresh basil, finely chopped

DRESSING:
½ cup extra-virgin olive oil
⅓ cup balsamic vinegar
1 teaspoon salt
½ teaspoon freshly ground black pepper

1. Put the orzo in a large pot of boiling water and allow to cook for 6 minutes.
2. Drain the orzo in a sieve and rinse well under cold running water. Set aside to cool completely.
3. When cooled, place the orzo in a large bowl. Add the olives, tomatoes, and basil. Toss well.
4. Mix together the olive oil, vinegar, pepper, and salt in a separate bowl. Pour the dressing into the bowl of orzo and vegetables. Toss gently to mix them thoroughly.
5. Serve chilled or at room temperature.

TIP: To add more flavors to this meal, serve it sprinkled with some freshly ground black pepper. And it tastes great paired with vegetable soups.

PER SERVING:
Calories: 480 | total fat: 28.3g | saturated fat: 4.2g | total carbs: 48.2g | fiber: 3.2g | protein: 8.1g | sugar: 2.8g | sodium: 850mg | cholesterol: 0mg

BULGUR WHEAT AND BROWNED ONIONS

Prep time: 10 minutes | Cook time: 35 minutes | Serves 6

½ cup olive oil
4 large chopped onions
2 teaspoons salt, divided
2 cups brown lentils, picked over and rinsed
6 cups water
1 cup bulgur wheat
1 teaspoon freshly ground black pepper

1. Heat the olive oil in a saucepan over medium heat. Add the onions and sauté for 3 to 4 minutes until the edges are lightly browned.
2. Season with 1 teaspoon of salt. Reserve half of the cooked onions on a platter for later use.
3. Add the remaining salt, lentils, and water to the remaining onions in the saucepan. Stir to combine and cook covered for about 20 to 25 minutes, stirring occasionally.
4. Fold in the bulgur wheat and sprinkle with the black pepper. Give it a good stir and cook for 5 minutes more. Using a fork to fluff the mixture, cover, and allow to sit for 5 minutes.
5. Remove from the saucepan to six serving plates. Serve topped with the reserved cooked onions.

TIP: This dish can be made ahead and kept in the refrigerator for no more than 5 days. You can serve it with a tomato and cucumber salad.

PER SERVING:
Calories: 485 | total fat: 20.4g | saturated fat: 2.8g | total carbs: 59.5g | fiber: 23.5g | protein: 20.1g | sugar: 6.8g | sodium: 788mg | cholesterol: 0mg

QUICK SPANISH RICE

Prep time: 10 minutes | Cook time: 15 minutes | Serves 4

2 tablespoons olive oil
1 medium onion, finely chopped
1 large tomato, finely diced
1 teaspoon smoked paprika
2 tablespoons tomato paste
1½ cups basmati rice
1 teaspoon salt
3 cups water

1. Heat the olive oil in a saucepan over medium heat. Add the onions and tomato and sauté for about 3 minutes until softened.
2. Add the paprika, tomato paste, basmati rice, and salt. Stir the mixture for 1 minute and slowly pour in the water.
3. Reduce the heat to low and allow to simmer covered for 12 minutes, stirring constantly.
4. Remove from the heat and let it rest in the saucepan for 3 minutes.
5. Divide the rice evenly among four serving bowls and serve.

TIP: For added color and twist, you can sprinkle with freshly chopped cilantro before serving.

PER SERVING:
Calories: 331 | total fat: 7.3g | saturated fat: 1.2g | total carbs: 59.8g | fiber: 2.1g | protein: 6.1g | sugar: 3.2g | sodium: 650mg | cholesterol: 0mg

RUSTIC LENTIL AND BASMATI RICE PILAF

Prep time: 5 minutes | Cook time: 50 minutes | Serves 6

¼ cup olive oil
1 large onion, chopped
1 teaspoon ground cumin
1 teaspoon salt
6 cups water
2 cups brown lentils, picked over and rinsed
1 cup basmati rice

1. Heat the olive oil in a saucepan over medium heat. Add the onions and cook for about 4 minutes until the onions are a medium golden color.
2. Turn the heat to high and add the cumin, salt, and water. Allow the mixture to boil for about 3 minutes until heated through.
3. Reduce the heat to medium-low and add the brown lentils. Allow to simmer covered for about 20 minutes until tender, stirring occasionally.
4. Add the basmati rice and stir well. Cook for 20 minutes until the rice has absorbed the liquid completely.
5. Using a fork to fluff the rice, cover, and let stand for 5 minutes.
6. Transfer to plates and serve hot.

TIP: This dish tastes great paired with tzatziki sauce, plain Greek yogurt, or green salads.

PER SERVING:
Calories: 400 | total fat: 11.3g | saturated fat: 1.1g | total carbs: 59.7g | fiber: 18g | protein: 18.4g | sugar: 3.9g | sodium: 397mg | cholesterol: 0mg

CREAMY POLENTA WITH PARMESAN CHEESE

Prep time: 5 minutes | Cook time: 25 minutes | Serves 4

3 tablespoons olive oil
1 tablespoon garlic, finely chopped
1 teaspoon salt
4 cups water
1 cup polenta
¾ cup Parmesan cheese, divided

1. In a large saucepan, heat the olive oil over medium heat.
2. Cook the garlic for 2 minutes until fragrant. Season with 1 teaspoon salt.
3. Pour in the water and bring it to a rapid boil. Fold in the polenta and stir for 3 minutes until it begins to thicken.
4. Reduce the heat to low, cover, and allow to simmer covered for about 20 minutes, whisking constantly.
5. Add the ½ cup of the Parmesan cheese and stir to combine.
6. Divide the polenta into four serving bowls and serve sprinkled with remaining cheese.

TIP: To add more flavors to this meal, you can serve it topped with freshly chopped parsley or basil. And it tastes great with grilled chicken breast or shrimp.

PER SERVING:
Calories: 300 | total fat: 15.8g | saturated fat: 10.1g | total carbs: 27.5g | fiber: 2.1g | protein: 8.7g | sugar: 0g | sodium: 835mg | cholesterol: 40mg

LEMON-HERBS ORZO

Prep time: 10 minutes | Cook time: 10 minutes | Serves 4

ORZO:
2 cups orzo
½ cup fresh basil, finely chopped
2 tablespoons lemon zest
½ cup fresh parsley, finely chopped

DRESSING:
½ cup extra-virgin olive oil
⅓ cup lemon juice
1 teaspoon salt
½ teaspoon freshly ground black pepper

1. Put the orzo in a large saucepan of boiling water and allow to cook for 6 minutes.
2. Drain the orzo in a sieve and rinse well under cold running water. Set aside to cool completely.
3. When cooled, place the orzo in a large bowl. Mix in the basil, lemon zest, and parsley. Set aside.
4. Make the dressing: In a separate bowl, combine the olive oil, lemon juice, salt, and pepper. Stir to incorporate.
5. Pour the dressing into the bowl of orzo mixture and toss gently until everything is well combined.
6. Serve immediately, or refrigerate for later.

TIP: It perfectly goes well with a barbecue or potluck, and you can add a can garbanzo beans (rinsed and drained) to add a protein kick.

PER SERVING:
Calories: 570 | total fat: 29.3g | saturated fat: 4.3g | total carbs: 65.1g | fiber: 4.2g | protein: 11.2g | sugar: 4.2g | sodium: 583mg | cholesterol: 0mg

Chapter 8 Sandwiches And Wraps

CITRUS CHICKEN SALAD IN LETTUCE WRAP

Prep time: 15 minutes | Cook time: 10 minutes | Serves 6

2 cups shredded chicken breasts
2 tablespoons Dijon mustard
Zest of 1 clementine or ½ small orange (about 1 tablespoon)
2 tablespoons fresh tarragon, chopped
½ cup plain Greek yogurt
2 tablespoons extra-virgin olive oil
½ teaspoon salt
¼ teaspoon freshly ground black pepper
½ cup almonds, slivered
6 large Bibb lettuce leaves, tough stem removed
2 small ripe avocados, peeled and thinly sliced

1. Add the shredded chicken breasts to a pot of water and bring to a boil. Boil for 10 minutes or until no longer pink.
2. Combine the Dijon mustard, clementine zest, tarragon, Greek yogurt, olive oil, salt, and black pepper in a bowl. Stir to combine well.
3. Dunk the cooked chicken and almonds in the bowl to coat well.
4. Make the lettuce wraps: Divide and spoon the chicken mixture in the center of each lettuce leaf, then spread the avocados on top before serving.

TIP: To make this a complete meal, you can serve it with vegan lasagna, and mushroom and artichokes pizza.

PER SERVING:
calories: 442 | total fat: 31.7g | total carbs: 12.2g | fiber: 7.8g | net carbs: 4.4g | protein: 26.1g | sodium: 443mg

GYROS WITH TZATZIKI

Prep time: 30 minutes | Cook time: 10 minutes | Serves 6

TZATZIKI:
1 medium cucumber, peeled, seeded, and grated
2 cups plain Greek yogurt
3 tablespoons lemon juice
4 mint leaves, chopped
4 cloves garlic, minced
½ teaspoon cumin
Salt and freshly ground pepper, to taste

MARINADE:
½ onion, quartered
½ teaspoon ground ginger
½ teaspoon cayenne pepper
1 tablespoon olive oil
1 teaspoon prepared mustard
1 teaspoon freshly ground black pepper
2 tablespoons sugar
3 cloves garlic
¼ cup water

1½ pounds (680 g) sirloin tip roast, cut into 1-inch strips
6 whole-wheat pita bread
2 tomatoes, chopped
1 red onion, thinly sliced
1 head romaine, cut into strips

1. Make the tzatziki: Combine all the ingredients for the tzatziki in a bowl. Stir to mix well and set aside until ready to serve.
2. Combine all the ingredients for the marinade in a blender. Process until smooth. Pour the marinade in a large bowl.
3. Dunk the sirloin in the marinade to coat well. Wrap the bowl in plastic and refrigerate to marinate for at least 4 hours.
4. Preheat the grill to HIGH. Remove the marinated sirloin from the refrigerator and place on the grill grate.
5. Grill the sirloin for 6 minutes. Flip the sirloin halfway through the cooking time or until well browned.
6. Remove the sirloin from the grill, then heat the pita bread on the grill until golden brown on both sides.
7. Divide the sirloin into the pitas, then slide the tomatoes, onion, and romaine in the pitas. Divide and spoon the tzatziki over the fillings and serve hot.

TIP: To make this a complete meal, you can serve it with potato chips and roasted asparagus salad.

PER SERVING:
calories: 258 | total fat: 5.4g | saturated fat: 1.1g | cholesterol: 73mg | total carbs: 17.7g | fiber: 4.2g | sugar: 8.0g | protein: 35.9g | sodium: 121mg

CUCUMBER SANDWICH WITH HUMMUS

Prep time: 20 minutes | Cook time: 0 minutes | Serves 2

4 slices whole-grain bread
¼ cup hummus
1 large cucumber, thinly sliced
4 whole basil leaves

1. Place slice of bread on a clean work surface, and spread with hummus, then put half of the cucumbers, and half of basil leaves on the hummus.
2. Assemble the sandwich with another slice of bread. Repeat to make another sandwich. Serve the sandwich immediately.

TIP: HOW TO MAKE HUMMUS:
1 (15-ounce / 425-g) can chickpeas, or 2 cups fresh chickpeas (If you have the can of chickpeas, then it can be used immediately; if you choose the fresh chickpeas, you'd better soak them in water for overnight to make them soft)

2 tablespoons extra-virgin olive oil
2 tablespoons tahini
Juice of ½ lemon
1 clove garlic, granulated
Salt and freshly ground black pepper, to taste

1. Add all ingredients in a food processor and process until creamy and smooth. Serve immediately or keep in the refrigerator for 3 to 5 days or in the freezer for 6 to 8 months.

PER SERVING:
calories: 216 | total fat: 4.9g | saturated fat: 0.8g | cholesterol: 0mg | total carbs: 33.6g | fiber: 5.1g | sugar: 2.9g | protein: 9.5g | sodium: 366mg

CHICKEN CUBES AND VEGETABLE PITA

Prep time: 15 minutes | Cook time: 20 minutes | Serves 2

4 tablespoons olive oil
1 boneless, skinless chicken breast
Salt and freshly ground pepper, to taste
½ small cucumber, chopped
½ small red onion, thinly sliced
1 tomato, chopped
1 cup baby spinach
1 roasted red pepper, sliced
Juice of 1 lemon
1 whole-wheat pita pocket
2 tablespoons feta cheese, crumbled

1. Preheat the grill to HIGH. Grease the grill grates with 2 tablespoons of olive oil.
2. On a clean work surface, rub the chicken breast with salt and pepper.
3. Place the seasoned chicken on the grill grate and grill for 15 minutes. Flip the chicken breast halfway through the cooking time or until lightly browned.
4. Meanwhile, combine all the vegetables in a large bowl, and sprinkle with salt and black pepper. Toss to mix well.
5. Remove the chicken from the grill, and allow to cool for a few minutes, then chop the chicken breast into cubes.
6. Add the chicken cubes to the bowl of vegetables, then drizzle with lemon juice and remaining olive oil. Toss to combine well.
7. Divide and slide the mixture in the pita pocket, then spread the feta cheese on top. Slice in half and serve immediately.

TIP: You can serve the pita with carrot sticks or French fries. It also tastes will paired with crab meat soup.

PER SERVING:
calories: 371 | total fat: 20.5g | saturated fat: 4.8g | cholesterol: 99mg | total carbs: 18.3g | fiber: 3.5g | sugar: 5.9g | protein: 31.9g | sodium: 350mg

TUNA SALAD SANDWICHES

Prep time: 15 minutes | Cook time: 5 minutes | Serves 2

6 ounces (170 g) white tuna, packed in water or olive oil, drained
1 roasted red pepper, diced
½ small red onion, diced
10 olives, pitted and finely chopped
¼ cup plain Greek yogurt
1 tablespoon flat-leaf parsley, chopped
Juice of 1 lemon
Salt and freshly ground pepper, to taste
1 tablespoon olive oil
4 whole-grain pieces of bread

1. Combine all the ingredients, except for the bread and olive oil, in a medium bowl. Stir to mix well.
2. Heat the olive oil in a nonstick skillet over medium-high heat.
3. Toast the bread in the skillet for 2 to 4 minutes or until golden brown. Flip the bread halfway through the cooking time.
4. Assemble the bread with the mixture to make the sandwich and serve warm.

TIP: To make this a complete meal, you can serve it with roasted chicken breasts or bacon-wrapped scallop.

PER SERVING:
calories: 398 | total fat: 11.6g | saturated fat: 1.9g | cholesterol: 29mg | total carbs: 36.3g | fiber: 5.4g | sugar: 7.7g | protein: 37.2g | sodium: 948mg

LUSCIOUS VEGAN PITA

Prep time: 15 minutes | Cook time: 20 minutes | Serves 2

½ small cucumber
½ cup alfalfa sprouts
½ cup button mushrooms, sliced
1 tomato, chopped
1 small red onion, thinly sliced
2 cups baby spinach leaves
Juice of 1 lemon
2 tablespoons olive oil
Sea salt and freshly ground pepper, to taste
2 whole-grain pita pockets

1. Mix all the vegetables, lemon juice, and olive oil in a large bowl, then sprinkle with salt and black pepper. Toss to combine well.
2. Divide and slide the vegetables in two pita pockets before serving.

TIP: You can serve the pita with carrot sticks or French fries. It also tastes will paired with scallop chowder.

PER SERVING:
calories: 241 | total fat: 14.7g | saturated fat: 2.1g | cholesterol: 0mg | total carbs: 25.6g | fiber: 4.9g | sugar: 4.7g | protein: 5.3g | sodium: 155mg

BROWN RICE AND ASPARAGUS TORTILLA WRAPS

Prep time: 15 minutes | Cook time: 55 minutes | Serves 6

2 cups brown rice
12 spears asparagus
1 ripe avocado, mashed
2 cloves garlic, minced
Juice of 1 lime
3 tablespoons Greek yogurt
Salt and freshly ground pepper, to taste
3 (8-inch) whole-grain tortillas
2 tablespoons red onion, diced
½ cup cilantro, diced

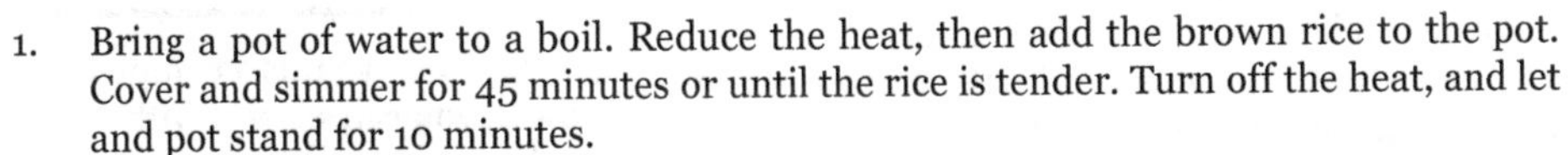

1. Bring a pot of water to a boil. Reduce the heat, then add the brown rice to the pot. Cover and simmer for 45 minutes or until the rice is tender. Turn off the heat, and let and pot stand for 10 minutes.
2. Bring another pot of water to a boil, then add the asparagus and cook for 1 to 3 minutes or until tender. Remove the asparagus from the pot and set aside.
3. Combine the avocado, garlic, and lime juice in a bowl. Combine the yogurt and cooked brown rice in another bowl. Season both mixtures with salt and pepper.
4. Heat the tortillas in the nonstick skillet until lightly browned on both sides.
5. Spoon two mixtures in the center of the tortillas, then spread the onion, cilantro, and asparagus on top.
6. Fold both sides of the tortillas up, then roll them up to close. Cut in half and serve warm.

TIP: You can prepare more cooked browned rice at one time for future use, or you can even use the leftover brown rice or cook in advance.

PER SERVING:
calories: 201 | total fat: 7.8g | saturated fat: 2.0g | cholesterol: 1mg | total carbs: 29.4g | fiber: 5.8g | sugar: 1.7g | protein: 5.0g | sodium: 115mg

Chapter 9 Pizza And Pasta

TOMATO LINGUINE

Prep time: 15 minutes | Cook time: 10 minutes | Serves 4

8 ounces (227 g) whole-grain linguine
1 tablespoon olive oil
¼ cup yellow onion, chopped
1 teaspoon fresh oregano, chopped
2 garlic cloves, minced
1 teaspoon tomato paste
½ teaspoon salt
¼ teaspoon freshly ground black pepper
8 ounces (227 g) cherry tomatoes, halved
½ cup Parmesan cheese, grated
1 tablespoon fresh parsley, chopped

1. Bring a pot of water to a boil over high heat. Add the linguine to the pot and cook 9 minutes or until al dente. Transfer the linguine to a plate, and reserve ½ cup of the linguine water.
2. Heat the olive oil in a nonstick skillet over medium-high heat.
3. Add the onion, oregano, and garlic to the skillet and sauté for 5 minutes until the onion is translucent.
4. Add the tomato paste, linguine water to the skillet, and sprinkle with salt and pepper. Stir to combine well and cook for 1 more minute.
5. Add the cooked linguine and cherry tomatoes, then sauté to coat well.
6. Slide the linguine in a large plate, and pour the sauce remains in the skillet over, then spread the cheese and parsley on top before serving.

TIP: To make this a complete meal, you can serve it with roasted Brussels sprouts and grilled chicken.

PER SERVING:
calories: 162 | total fat: 9.1g | saturated fat: 2.7g | cholesterol: 11mg | total carbs: 15.1g | fiber: 2.8g | sugar: 3.7g | protein: 6.2g | sodium: 665mg

GREEK FLAVOR TOMATO CHICKEN PASTA

Prep time: 20 minutes | Cook time: 3 hours 20minutes | Serves 4

3 tablespoons olive oil
1 pound (454 g) boneless, skinless chicken breasts, cut into 1-inch cubes
15 ounces (425 g) tomatoes, diced
2 medium carrots, thinly sliced
1½ cups freshly squeezed tomato juice
1½ cups low-sodium chicken broth
1 stalk celery, finely chopped
1 medium onion, cut into wedges
½ teaspoon rosemary
½ teaspoon thyme
1 teaspoon basil
1 teaspoon oregano
½ teaspoon ground cinnamon
½ teaspoon sea salt
1 cup uncooked medium shell pasta
1 cup feta cheese, crumbled

1. Coat the insert of the slow cooker with 2 tablespoons olive oil.
2. Heat the remaining olive oil in a nonstick skillet over medium-high heat.
3. Add the chicken to the skillet and cook for 6 minutes until lightly browned on all sides. Shake the skillet periodically during the cooking.
4. Transfer the chicken to a plate, and pat dry with paper towels, then move them into the slow cooker.
5. Add the tomatoes, carrots, tomato juice, chicken stock, celery, and onion to the slow cooker. Season with rosemary, thyme, basil, oregano, cinnamon, and salt. Stir to mix well.
6. Put the slow cooker lid on and cook on HIGH for 2 hours and 30 minutes.
7. Add the pasta to the slow cooker. Put the lid on and cook for an additional 40 minutes or until the pasta is al dente.
8. Serve the pasta, chicken, and vegetables on a large plate, and spread the feta cheese on top before serving.

TIP: To make this a complete meal, you can serve it with spinach and mushroom salad.

PER SERVING:
calories: 581 | total fat: 32.4g | saturated fat: 11.6g | cholesterol: 87mg | total carbs: 47.9g | fiber: 5.0g | sugar: 10.8g | protein: 29.4g | sodium: 1309mg

ITALIAN FLAVOR RICOTTA AND TOMATO PIZZA

Prep time: 15 minutes | Cook time: 30 minutes | Serves 2

½ cup balsamic vinegar
1 cup chickpea flour
½ teaspoon onion powder
½ teaspoon garlic powder
1 teaspoon baking powder
2 tablespoons Parmesan cheese, grated
1½ teaspoons Italian seasoning herb mix, divided
½ teaspoon salt
¾ cup warm water
1 tablespoon olive oil
½ cup ricotta cheese
1 ripe tomato, thinly sliced

1. Make the balsamic glaze: Pour the balsamic vinegar in a saucepan, then bring to a boil. Turn down the heat to low and simmer for another 10 minutes or until it reduces in half and can coat the back of a spoon. Set aside until ready to serve.
2. Preheat the oven to 425°F (220°C).
3. Combine the chickpea flour, onion powder, garlic powder, baking powder, Parmesan, 1 teaspoon of Italian seasoning herb mix, and salt in a bowl.
4. Pour ¾ cup of water in the bowl, then stir to mix well until it forms a lightly thickened batter.
5. Heat the olive oil in an oven-safe skillet over medium-high heat.
6. Make the crust: Pour the batter in the skillet. Level with a spatula and cook for 1 minute until it starts to bubble, then move the skillet in the preheated oven and cook for 10 minutes or until the batter is golden brown and the edges start to set.
7. Meanwhile, combine the ricotta cheese with remaining Italian seasoning herb mix.
8. Remove the skillet from the oven. Scatter with the ricotta mixture, then spread the tomatoes on top.
9. Move the skillet back to the oven and cook for 2 more minutes until the cheese melts.
10. Transfer the pizza to a large serving plate, then serve with balsamic glaze on top.

TIP: To make this a complete meal, you can serve it with roasted shrimp with feta white beans.

PER SERVING:
calories: 319 | total fat: 9.8g | total carbs: 37.2g | fiber: 6.2g | sugar: 9.1g | protein: 20.1g | sodium: 761mg

ZUCCHINI, TOMATO, AND PINE NUT FARFALLE

Prep time: 15 minutes | Cook time: 25 minutes | Serves 6

2 pounds (907 g) zucchini, halved lengthwise and sliced ½ inch thick
Salt and freshly ground black pepper, to taste
5 tablespoons olive oil, divided
3 garlic cloves, minced
½ teaspoon red pepper flakes
1 pound (454 g) farfalle
12 ounces (340 g) grape tomatoes, halved
½ cup fresh basil, chopped
¼ cup pine nuts, toasted
2 tablespoons balsamic vinegar
½ cup Parmesan cheese, grated

1. Put the zucchini in a large bowl, and sprinkle with 1 tablespoon of salt. Let stand for 30 minutes, then pat dry with paper towels.
2. Warm 1 tablespoon of olive oil in a nonstick skillet over high heat until shimmering.
3. Add the zucchini to the skillet and sauté for 6 minutes until tender. Reserve the zucchini in a separate bowl.
4. Warm 1 tablespoon olive oil in the cleaned skillet over medium heat.
5. Add the garlic and red pepper flakes and sauté for 30 seconds until fragrant.
6. Add the cooked zucchini and sauté for 30 seconds to warm through.
7. Bring a pot of 4 quarts of water to a boil. Add the farfalle to the pot, and sprinkle with 1 tablespoon salt. Cook for 11 minutes until al dente. Stir constantly.
8. Spoon ½ cup of farfalle water into a small bowl to reserve until ready to use. Remove the farfalle from the pot to a plate, and pat dry with paper towels.
9. Add the cooked zucchini, tomatoes, pine nuts, vinegar, basil and remaining olive oil to the plate, then sprinkle with salt and black pepper. Toss to combine well.
10. Pour over the reserved farfalle water and scatter with Parmesan cheese before serving.

TIP: To make this a complete meal, you can serve it with creamy fish soup and grilled chicken wings.

PER SERVING:
calories: 320 | total fat: 20.8g | total carbs: 27.0g | fiber: 5.5g | sugar: 10.9g | protein: 11.8g | sodium: 332mg

SPAGHETTI AL LIMONE

Prep time: 15 minutes | Cook time: 10 minutes | Serves 6

1 (2-ounce / 57-g) Parmesan cheese, grated
⅓ cup lemon juice
2 teaspoons lemon zest
1 small garlic clove, minced
2 tablespoons extra-virgin olive oil
Salt and freshly ground black pepper, to taste
1 pound (454 g) spaghetti
6 tablespoons fresh basil, shredded

1. Combine the Parmesan, lemon juice and zest, garlic, olive oil, ½ teaspoon of salt, and ¼ teaspoon of pepper in a blender. Process until smooth and creamy. Set aside.
2. Pour a gallon of water in a pot, and bring to a boil. Sprinkle with 1 tablespoon of salt, and add the spaghetti to the pot. Cook according to the package direction until al dente. Stir constantly during the cooking.
3. Transfer the cooked spaghetti to a large plate, and pat day with paper towels. Reserve ½ cup of spaghetti water.
4. Pour the lemon mixture over the spaghetti, then sprinkle with basil. Toss to coat well. Use the reserved spaghetti water to adjust the consistency before serving.

TIP: To make this a complete meal, you can serve it with grilled salmon or bacon-wrapped scallop.

PER SERVING:
calories: 184 | total fat: 7.7g | saturated fat: 2.2g | cholesterol: 8mg | total carbs: 22.7g | fiber: 3.5g | sugar: 1.0g | protein: 6.9g | sodium: 173mg

EASY TOMATO AND EGG PIZZA

Prep time: 5 minutes | Cook time: 15 minutes | Serves 2

1 tablespoon olive oil
2 pieces large whole-wheat naan
2 tablespoons pesto
1 medium tomato, sliced
2 large eggs

1. Warm the olive oil in a nonstick skillet over medium-high heat.
2. Add the naan and heat for 4 minutes. Flip the naan halfway through or until golden brown.
3. Brush the pesto on one side of each naan piece, then put the tomato slices over the pesto. Transfer the naan onto two serving plates.
4. Separate the eggs in the same skillet, then fry for 7 minutes on both sides or until the egg whites are opaque and the yolks are set.
5. Slide the fried eggs on each naan before serving.

TIP: You can serve this dish as breakfast with plain Greek yogurt.

PER SERVING:
calories: 338 | total fat: 15.3g | saturated fat: 3.3g | cholesterol: 189mg | total carbs: 38.6g | fiber: 5.6g | sugar: 2.5g | protein: 14.7g | sodium: 503mg

ANCHOVIES AND BROCCOLI PENNE

Prep time: 15 minutes | Cook time: 20 minutes | Serves 4

1 pound (454 g) whole-wheat penne
2 tablespoons olive oil
4 anchovy fillets, packed in olive oil
½ pound (227 g) broccoli, cut into 1-inch florets
2 cloves garlic, sliced
¼ cup Parmesan cheese, grated
Red pepper flakes, to taste
Salt and freshly ground pepper, to taste

1. Bring a pot of water to a boil over high heat. Add the penne to the pot and cook for 8 to 12 minutes according to the package directions until al dente.
2. Warm the olive oil in a nonstick skillet over medium heat.
3. Add the anchovies, broccoli, and garlic to the skillet and sauté for 5 minutes or until fork-tender. Turn off the heat.
4. Transfer the cooked penne to a plate, and pat dry with paper towels, then add it to the skillet and stir to coat well.
5. Transfer them to a large plate and sprinkle with grated Parmesan cheese, red pepper flakes, salt, and pepper before serving.

TIP: To make this a complete meal, you can serve it with grilled zucchini salad.

PER SERVING:
calories: 307 | total fat: 8.1g | saturated fat: 0.3g | cholesterol: 3mg | total carbs: 33.7g | fiber: 7.0g | sugar: 1.7g | protein: 9.4g | sodium: 170mg

Chapter 10 Fish And Seafood

TROUT WITH SAUTÉED VEGETABLES

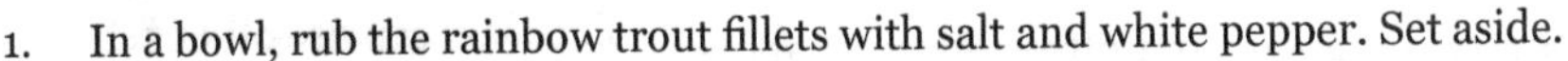

Prep time: 10 minutes | Cook time: 20 minutes | Serves 4

2 pounds (907 g) rainbow trout fillets
Salt and ground white pepper, to taste
1 tablespoon olive oil
1 pound (454 g) asparagus
4 medium golden potatoes, thinly sliced
1 garlic clove, finely minced
1 scallion, thinly sliced, green and white parts separated
2 Roma tomatoes, chopped
1 large carrot, thinly sliced
8 pitted kalamata olives, chopped
¼ cup ground cumin
2 tablespoons paprika
2 tablespoons dried parsley
1 tablespoon vegetable bouillon seasoning
½ cup dry white wine

1. In a bowl, rub the rainbow trout fillets with salt and white pepper. Set aside.
2. Heat the olive oil in a large skillet over medium heat. Sauté the asparagus, golden potatoes, garlic, and the white parts of the scallion in the oil for about 5 minutes, stirring occasionally, or until the garlic is fragrant.
3. Toss in the tomatoes, carrot slices and olives, then continue to cook until the vegetables are tender but still crisp, about 5 to 7 minutes.
4. Add the cumin, paprika, parsley, vegetable bouillon seasoning, and salt. Stir to combine well. Top with the seasoned fillets and slowly pour in the white wine.
5. Turn the heat down to low, cover, and bring to a simmer for about 6 minutes, or until the flesh is opaque and it flakes apart easily.
6. Remove from the heat and sprinkle the scallion greens on top for garnish before serving.

TIP: If you don't want to cook the whole trout fillets at a time, you can cut them into uniform pieces and cover with plastic wrap, then put in the freezer for next meal.

PER SERVING:
Calories: 495 | total fat: 19.3g | saturated fat: 5.2g | total carbs: 41.2g | fiber: 7.1g | protein: 40.2g | sugar: 8.1g | sodium: 732mg | cholesterol: 110mg

SHRIMP WITH BLACK BEAN PASTA

Prep time: 10 minutes | Cook time: 15 minutes | Serves 4

1 package black bean pasta
4 tablespoons olive oil
3 garlic cloves, minced
1 onion, finely chopped
1 pound (454 g) fresh shrimp, peeled and deveined
Salt and pepper, to taste
¾ cup low-sodium chicken broth
¼ cup basil, cut into strips

1. Put the black bean pasta in a large pot of boiling water and cook for 6 minutes.
2. Remove the pasta from the heat. Drain and rinse with cold water, then set the pasta aside on a platter.
3. Heat the olive oil in a large skillet over medium heat. Add the garlic and onion, then cook for 3 minutes until the onion is translucent.
4. Add the shrimp and season with salt and pepper. Cook for 3 minutes, stirring occasionally, or until the shrimp is opaque. Pour in the chicken broth and let it simmer for 2 to 3 minutes until heated through.
5. Remove the shrimp from the heat to the platter of pasta. Pour the liquid over the pasta and garnish with basil, then serve.

TIP: If the black bean pasta is not available, you can try any of your favorite pasta with this recipe. And for a unique twist, the jumbo lump crab meat can be substituted for shrimp.

PER SERVING:
Calories: 670 | total fat: 19.2g | saturated fat: 2.2g | total carbs: 73.3g | fiber: 31.2g | protein: 57.2g | sugar: 1.1g | sodium: 610mg | cholesterol: 225mg

SPANISH STYLE SALMON WITH VEGETABLES

Prep time: 10 minutes | Cook time: 20 minutes | Serves 4

2 small red onions, thinly sliced
1 cup shaved fennel bulbs
1 cup cherry tomatoes
15 green pimiento-stuffed olives
1 teaspoon cumin seeds
½ teaspoon smoked paprika
Salt and freshly ground black pepper, to taste
4 (8-ounce / 227-g) salmon fillets
½ cup chicken broth, low-sodium
2 to 4 tablespoons olive oil
2 cups cooked couscous

1. Preheat the oven to 375°F (190°C).
2. Arrange the red onions, fennel bulbs, cherry tomatoes, and olives on two baking sheets. Sprinkle with cumin seeds, paprika, salt, and pepper.
3. Place the salmon fillets on top of the vegetables and sprinkle with salt. Pour the chicken broth evenly over the two baking sheets and drizzle with olive oil.
4. Bake in the preheated oven for 18 to 20 minutes until the vegetables are tender and the fish is flaky, checking regularly to ensure they don't overcook.
5. Divide the cooked couscous among four serving plates and top with vegetables and fillets, then serve.

TIP: If you can't find the salmon fillets, you can use other fish of your choice, like swordfish. The leftovers can be stored for salmon patties.

PER SERVING:
Calories: 480 | total fat: 18.3g | saturated fat: 3.2g | total carbs: 26.2g | fiber: 3.1g | protein: 50.2g | sugar: 3.2g | sodium: 295mg | cholesterol: 168mg

SWORDFISH WITH LEMON AND TARRAGON

Prep time: 5 minutes | Cook time: 15 minutes | Serves 4

1 pound (454 g) swordfish steaks, cut into 2-inch pieces
1 teaspoon salt, or more to taste
¼ teaspoon freshly ground black pepper
¼ cup olive oil and plus 2 tablespoons, divided
2 tablespoons unsalted butter
2 tablespoons fresh tarragon, chopped
Zest and juice of 1 lemon
Zest and juice of 2 clementines

1. Season the swordfish steaks with salt and pepper in a bowl.
2. Heat ¼ cup olive oil in a large skillet over medium-high heat. Sear the swordfish steaks for 2 to 3 minutes per side until lightly browned.
3. With a slotted spoon, remove the swordfish steaks from the heat to a plate.
4. Add 2 tablespoons olive oil and butter to the skillet over medium-low heat.
5. When the butter melts, fold in the tarragon, lemon and clementine zests and juices. Season with salt and stir well.
6. Return the swordfish steaks to the skillet. Cook for about 2 minutes more and let the swordfish steaks coat in the sauce thoroughly.
7. Remove from the heat and serve on plates.

TIP: You can try fresh sea scallops with this recipe and it tastes great paired with riced cauliflower or sautéed greens.

PER SERVING:
Calories: 383 | total fat: 31.2g | saturated fat: 7.5g | total carbs: 3.2g | fiber: 0g | protein: 23.2g | sodium: 726mg

STUFFED SQUID WITH SPINACH AND CHEESE

Prep time: 15 minutes | Cook time: 30 minutes | Serves 4

4 tablespoons olive oil, divided

FILLING:
¼ cup olive oil
8 ounces (227 g) frozen spinach, thawed and drained
¼ cup sun-dried tomatoes, chopped
½ cup chopped pitted olives
4 ounces (113 g) goat cheese, crumbled
2 garlic cloves, finely minced
¼ cup fresh flat-leaf Italian parsley, chopped
¼ teaspoon freshly ground black pepper

2 pounds (907 g) baby squid, cleaned and tentacles removed

Preheat the oven to 350°F (180°C). Coat the bottom of a baking dish with 2 tablespoons olive oil and set aside.
Make the filling: Mix together ¼ cup olive oil, spinach, tomatoes, olives, goat cheese, garlic, parsley, and pepper in a bowl until well combined.
On a clean work surface, spoon 2 tablespoons of the filling onto each baby squid, then arrange them on the prepared baking dish. Evenly pour the remaining olive oil over the squid.
Bake in the preheated oven for 25 to 30 minutes until cooked through.
Remove from the oven and cool for 8 minutes before serving.

TIP: If you can't find the baby squid, you can replace it with calamari steaks, but don't remember to increase the cook time.

PER SERVING:
Calories: 473 | total fat: 37.4g | total carbs: 7.3g | fiber: 3.3g | protein: 24.3g | sodium: 578mg

MEDITERRANEAN SHEET PAN FISH FILLETS

Prep time: 10 minutes | Cook time: 10 minutes | Serves 4

4 (4-ounce/ 113-g) fish fillets, such as cod or tilapia (½ inch thick)
2 tablespoons olive oil
1 tablespoon balsamic vinegar
2½ cups (about 12 ounces) green beans
1 pint (about 2 cups) cherry or grape tomatoes
Nonstick cooking spray

1. Preheat the oven to 400°F (205°C). Spray two large baking sheets with nonstick cooking spray.
2. Arrange two fish fillets on each baking sheet and set aside.
3. Stir together the olive oil and vinegar in a bowl.
4. In a separate bowl, mix the green beans and tomatoes. Pour the olive oil and vinegar mixture into the bowl of vegetables. Toss gently to coat the vegetables in the mixture.
5. Divide the coated vegetables among the fish fillets and pour over the mixture.
6. Bake in the preheated oven for 5 to 8 minutes, or until the flesh is opaque and it flakes apart easily.
7. Allow to cool for 5 minutes and serve hot.

TIP: For additional zest, you can add a sprinkle of lemon juice and chopped parsley. You also can serve it with sautéed zucchini.

PER SERVING:
Calories: 245 | total fat: 14.3g | saturated fat: 5.2g | total carbs: 5.3g | fiber: 2.3g | protein: 22.1g | sugar: 2.1g | sodium: 135mg | phosphorus: 244mg | potassium: 530mg | cholesterol: 57mg

QUICK MUSSELS WITH WHITE WINE SAUCE

Prep time: 5 minutes | Cook time: 10 minutes | Serves 4

2 pounds (907 g) small mussels
1 tablespoon olive oil
3 garlic cloves, sliced
1 cup thinly sliced red onion (about ½ medium onion)
2 (¼-inch-thick) lemon slices
1 cup dry white wine
¼ teaspoon kosher or sea salt
¼ teaspoon freshly ground black pepper
Fresh lemon wedges, for garnish

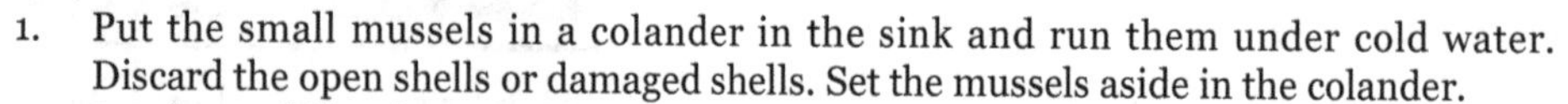

1. Put the small mussels in a colander in the sink and run them under cold water. Discard the open shells or damaged shells. Set the mussels aside in the colander.
2. In a large skillet, heat the olive oil over medium-high heat. Add the garlic and onion, cook for 3 to 4 minutes until tender, stirring occasionally.
3. Add the lemon slices, wine, salt, and pepper. Stir well and allow to simmer for 2 minutes.
4. Pour in the mussels and cook covered until the mussels open their shells, giving the pan a shake from time to time, about 3 minutes.
5. With a slotted spoon, transfer the mussels to a serving bowl. Be sure to discard any mussels that are still closed.
6. Pour the wine sauce over the mussels in the bowl and serve garnished with lemon wedges.

TIP: To make this a complete meal, you can serve it with garlic bread or lemony broth on the side.

PER SERVING:
Calories: 344 | total fat: 16.3g | saturated fat: 5.8g | total carbs: 11.5g | fiber: 0g | protein: 36.4g | sugar: 1.1g | sodium: 1270mg | phosphorus: 585mg | potassium: 833mg | cholesterol: 92mg

MARINATED SHRIMP WITH ORANGE

Prep time: 10 minutes | Cook time: 10 minutes | Serves 6

1½ pounds (680 g) fresh raw shrimp, shells and tails removed
3 tablespoons olive oil, divided
1 large orange, zested and peeled
3 garlic cloves, minced
1 tablespoon chopped fresh thyme (about 6 sprigs)
1 tablespoon chopped fresh rosemary (about 3 sprigs)
¼ teaspoon kosher or sea salt
¼ teaspoon freshly ground black pepper

1. Put the shrimp, 2 tablespoons olive oil, orange zest, garlic, thyme, rosemary, salt, and pepper in a zip-top plastic bag. Seal the bag and shake until the shrimp is coated thoroughly. Set aside to marinate for 5 minutes.
2. In a large skillet, heat 1 tablespoon olive oil over medium heat. Add the shrimp and cook for 2 to 3 minutes per side, or until the flesh is totally pink and opaque.
3. Meanwhile, slice the peeled orange into bite-sized wedges on your cutting board, then place in a serving bowl.
4. Remove the shrimp from the pan to the bowl. Toss well. Serve immediately, or refrigerate to chill until you want to serve.

TIP: The orange zest can be replaced with lemon zest. For a distinct combination, you can use ¼ cup freshly chopped mint substituted for the thyme and rosemary in this recipe.

PER SERVING:
Calories: 144 | total fat: 8.3g | saturated fat: 1.1g | total carbs: 3g | fiber: 0.1g | protein: 23.4g | sugar: 1.8g | sodium: 1084mg | phosphorus: 227mg | potassium: 137mg | cholesterol: 286mg

POACHED SALMON WITH MUSTARD SAUCE

Prep time: 15 minutes | Cook time: 20 minutes | Serves 2

MUSTARD SAUCE:

¼ cup plain Greek yogurt
2 tablespoons Dijon mustard
1½ teaspoons dried tarragon
Pinch salt
Pinch freshly ground black pepper

SALMON:

10 ounces (284 g) salmon fillets
1 tablespoon olive oil
Salt and freshly ground black pepper, to taste
½ fresh lemon, sliced
¼ cup dry white wine
Juice of ½ lemon
¼ cup water

1. Make the mustard sauce: In a bowl, mix together the yogurt, Dijon mustard, tarragon, salt, and pepper until well combined. Set aside.
2. In a separate bowl, brush the salmon fillets with olive oil, salt, and pepper. Place the lemon slices on top of the fillets.
3. Add the white wine, lemon juice, and water to a skillet over medium-high heat. Bring them to a boil, then put in the salmon fillets.
4. Reduce the heat to medium and allow to simmer covered for 15 minutes, or until the fish is flaky.
5. Divide the salmon fillets between two serving plates. Pour the mustard sauce over the fillets, then serve warm.

TIP: You can try other fresh herbs of your choice, such as thyme, oregano or rosemary.

PER SERVING:
Calories: 330 | total fat: 21.2g | total carbs: 3.2g | fiber: 0g | protein: 22.2g | sugar: 2.1g | sodium: 443mg | cholesterol: 70mg

GRILLED HALIBUT WITH ROMESCO SAUCE

Prep time: 20 minutes | Cook time: 10 minutes | Serves 2

ROMESCO SAUCE:

½ cup jarred roasted piquillo peppers
¼ cup raw and unsalted almonds
2 tablespoons sun-dried tomatoes in olive oil with herbs
¼ teaspoon smoked paprika , or more to taste
2 small garlic cloves
¼ cup olive oil
2 tablespoons red wine vinegar
Pinch salt

HALIBUT:

2 (5-ounce / 142-g) halibut steaks
1 tablespoon olive oil, for greasing the grill grates
Salt and freshly ground black pepper, to taste

1. Make the romesco sauce: In a food processor, put the piquillo peppers, almonds, tomatoes, paprika, garlic cloves, olive oil, vinegar, and salt. Pulse until all ingredients are combined into a smooth mixture. Transfer to a bowl and set aside.
2. Preheat the grill to medium-high heat. Lightly grease the grill grates with olive oil and set aside.
3. In a separate bowl, rub the halibut steaks with olive oil, salt, and pepper.
4. Grill the halibut steaks on the preheated grill for about 10 minutes, flipping the steaks halfway through, or until the fish flakes easily with a fork and juices run clear.
5. Transfer the halibut steaks to two plates and pour over the romesco sauce. Serve hot.

TIP: You can store the remaining Romesco sauce in a sealed airtight container in the fridge for up to one week.

PER SERVING:
Calories: 266 | total fat: 13.2g | total carbs: 3.2g | fiber: 1.1g | protein: 31.2g | sugar: 1.1g | sodium: 107mg | cholesterol: 0mg

MACKEREL NIÇOISE SALAD

Prep time: 10 minutes | Cook time: 20 minutes | Serves 2

DRESSING:

4 tablespoons olive oil
3 tablespoons red wine vinegar
1 teaspoon Dijon mustard
¼ teaspoon salt
Pinch freshly ground black pepper

SALAD:

2 teaspoons salt
2 small red potatoes
1 cup green beans
2 cups baby greens
2 hard-boiled eggs, sliced
½ cup cherry tomatoes, halved
⅓ cup Niçoise olives
2 (4-ounce / 113-g) cooked mackerel fillets

1. Make the dressing: In a bowl, combine the olive oil, vinegar, mustard, salt, and pepper. Stir with a fork until mixed completely and set aside.
2. Make the salad: Fill a large pot with 3 inches of cold water, and add the salt. Bring it to a boil, then add the red potatoes and cook until they can be pierced easily with the tip of a sharp knife but are still firm, about 12 minutes.
3. Remove the red potatoes from the heat to a colander. Blanch the green beans in the boiling water for 5 minutes, or until they start to soften. Transfer the green beans to the colander of potatoes. Let them cool under running cold water. When cooled, drain and dry with paper towels, then slice the potatoes on a flat work surface.
4. Spread out the baby greens on two serving plates. Top each plate with the sliced potatoes, green beans, and hard-boiled eggs. Scatter the tomatoes and olives over them, then place the mackerel fillets on top of the salad.
5. To serve, pour the prepared dressing over the salad and toss well.

TIP: To save time, you can buy the canned mackerel fillets directly in the market. And you can try any of your favorite fish, like grilled salmon or canned tuna.

PER SERVING:
Calories: 660 | total fat:47.3 g | total carbs: 38.5g | fiber: 7.2g | protein: 25.3g | sugar: 4.1g | sodium: 350mg | cholesterol: 160mg

TIP: To add more flavors to this meal, serve it alongside the broccoli salad with toasted walnuts. It also tastes great paired with the garlic aioli.

PER SERVING:
Calories: 340 | total fat: 26.3g | total carbs: 5.2g | fiber: 1.1g | protein: 23.2g | sodium: 693mg

BROWNED SALMON CAKES

Prep time: 15 minutes | Cook time: 15 minutes | Serves 4

1 pound (454 g) salmon fillets, spine, bones and skin removed
½ cup red onion, minced
1 large egg, whisked
2 tablespoons mayonnaise
1 ripe avocado, pitted, peeled, and mashed
½ cup almond flour
1 teaspoon garlic powder
1 to 2 teaspoons dried dill
½ teaspoon paprika
1 teaspoon salt
½ teaspoon freshly ground black pepper
Zest and juice of 1 lemon
¼ cup olive oil

1. On a clean work surface, cut the salmon fillets into small pieces and transfer to a large bowl.
2. Add the minced red onion to the bowl and mash the salmon with a fork to break up any lumps. Add the whisked egg, mayo, and mashed avocado. Stir to combine well and set aside.
3. In a separate bowl, mix together the almond flour, garlic powder, dill, paprika, salt, and pepper.
4. Pour the dry ingredients into the bowl of salmon mixture, along with the lemon zest and juice. Mix well.
5. Make the salmon cakes: Scoop out equal-sized portions of the salmon mixture and shape into patties with your palm, about 2 inches in diameter. Set aside on a plate for 15 minutes.
6. Heat the olive oil in a large skillet over medium heat. Add the salmon patties and fry for 2 to 3 minutes on each side until the edges are lightly browned. Reduce the heat to low and cook covered until the patties are cooked through, about 7 minutes.
7. Remove from the heat and serve on plates.

GARLICKY BRANZINO WITH FRESH HERBS

Prep time: 10 minutes | Cook time: 20 minutes | Serves 2

1½ pounds (680 g) branzino, scaled and gutted
Salt and freshly ground black pepper, to taste
1 tablespoon olive oil
1 sliced lemon
3 minced garlic cloves
¼ cup chopped fresh herbs (any mixture of thyme, oregano, rosemary, and parsley)

1. Preheat the oven to 425°F (220°C).
2. Arrange the branzino on a baking dish. Using a sharp knife, make 4 slits in the fish, about 1½ inches apart.
3. Generously brush the fish inside and out with salt and pepper, then drizzle with 1 tablespoon olive oil.
4. Place the lemon slices, garlic gloves, and fresh herbs into the cavity of the fish.
5. Roast the fish in the preheated oven for 15 to 20 minutes, or until the fish flakes easily with a fork and juices run clear.
6. Allow to cool for 5 minutes and remove the lemon slices before serving.

TIP: To make this a complete meal, serve it with sautéed mushroom and green beans as a side dish.

PER SERVING:
Calories: 290 | total fat: 12.3g | total carbs: 2.2g | fiber: 0g | protein: 42.3g | sugar: 0g | sodium: 150mg | cholesterol: 92mg

Chapter 11 Vegetarian Mains

MUSHROOM AND CHEESE STUFFED TOMATOES

Prep time: 15 minutes | Cook time: 20 minutes | Serves 4

4 large ripe tomatoes
1 tablespoon olive oil
½ pound (454 g) white or cremini mushrooms, sliced
1 tablespoon fresh basil, chopped
½ cup yellow onion, diced
1 tablespoon fresh oregano, chopped
2 garlic cloves, minced
½ teaspoon salt
¼ teaspoon freshly ground black pepper
1 cup part-skim Mozzarella cheese, shredded
1 tablespoon Parmesan cheese, grated

1. Preheat the oven to 375°F (190°C).
2. Cut a ½-inch slice off the top of each tomato. Scoop the pulp into a bowl and leave ½-inch tomato shells. Arrange the tomatoes on a baking sheet lined with aluminum foil.
3. Heat the olive oil in a nonstick skillet over medium heat.
4. Add the mushrooms, basil, onion, oregano, garlic, salt, and black pepper to the skillet and sauté for 5 minutes or until the mushrooms are soft.
5. Pour the mixture to the bowl of tomato pulp, then add the Mozzarella cheese and stir to combine well.
6. Spoon the mixture into each tomato shell, then top with a layer of Parmesan.
7. Bake in the preheated oven for 15 minutes or until the cheese is frothy and the tomatoes are soft.
8. Remove the stuffed tomatoes from the oven and serve warm.

TIP: To make this a complete meal, you can serve it with roasted Brussels sprouts with bacon.

PER SERVING:
calories: 254 | total fat: 14.7g | saturated fat: 6.7g | cholesterol: 37mg | total carbs: 15.8g | fiber: 5.2g | sugars: 7.4g | protein: 17.5g | sodium: 677mg

TABBOULEH

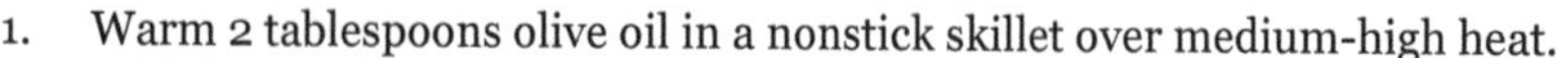

Prep time: 15 minutes | Cook time: 5 minutes | Serves 6

4 tablespoons olive oil, divided
4 cups riced cauliflower
3 garlic cloves, finely minced
Salt and freshly ground black pepper, to taste
½ large cucumber, peeled, seeded, and chopped
½ cup Italian parsley, chopped
Juice of 1 lemon
2 tablespoons minced red onion
½ cup mint leaves, chopped
½ cup pitted Kalamata olives, chopped
1 cup cherry tomatoes, quartered
2 cups baby arugula or spinach leaves
2 medium avocados, peeled, pitted, and diced

1. Warm 2 tablespoons olive oil in a nonstick skillet over medium-high heat.
2. Add the riced cauliflower, garlic, salt, and black pepper to the skillet and sauté for 3 minutes or until fragrant. Transfer them to a large bowl.
3. Add the cucumber, parsley, lemon juice, red onion, mint, olives, and remaining olive oil to the bowl. Toss to combine well. Reserve the bowl in the refrigerator for at least 30 minutes.
4. Remove the bowl from the refrigerator. Add the cherry tomatoes, arugula, avocado to the bowl. Sprinkle with salt and black pepper, and toss to combine well. Serve chilled.

TIP: To make this a complete meal, you can serve it with mushroom and chicken broth, or scallop chowder.

PER SERVING:
calories: 198 | total fat: 17.5g | total carbs: 12.1g | fiber: 6.2g | net carbs: 5.9g | protein: 4.2g | sodium: 621mg

SPICY BROCCOLI RABE AND ARTICHOKE HEARTS

Prep time: 5 minutes | Cook time: 15 minutes | Serves 4

3 tablespoons olive oil, divided
2 pounds (907 g) fresh broccoli rabe, stems removed and cut into florets
3 garlic cloves, finely minced
1 teaspoon red pepper flakes
1 teaspoon salt, plus more to taste
13.5 ounces (383 g) artichoke hearts, drained and quartered
1 tablespoon water
2 tablespoons red wine vinegar
Freshly ground black pepper, to taste

1. Warm 2 tablespoons olive oil in a nonstick skillet over medium-high skillet.
2. Add the broccoli, garlic, red pepper flakes, and salt to the skillet and sauté for 5 minutes or until the broccoli is soft.
3. Add the artichoke hearts to the skillet and sauté for 2 more minutes or until tender.
4. Add water to the skillet and turn down the heat to low. Put the lid on and simmer for 5 minutes.
5. Meanwhile, combine the vinegar and 1 tablespoon of olive oil in a bowl.
6. Drizzle the simmered broccoli and artichokes with oiled vinegar, and sprinkle with salt and black pepper. Toss to combine well before serving.

TIP: You can replace the broccoli rabe to leek or cabbage to change the palate of this recipe, or you can roast the artichoke in advance and sprinkle with chopped jalapeño for a stronger flavor.

PER SERVING:
calories: 272 | total fat: 21.5g | total carbs: 18.1g | fiber: 9.8g | net carbs: 8.3g | protein: 11.2g | sodium: 916mg

SHAKSHUKA

Prep time: 10 minutes | Cook time: 25 minutes | Serves 4

5 tablespoons olive oil, divided
1 red bell pepper, finely diced
½ small yellow onion, finely diced
14 ounces (397 g) crushed tomatoes, with juices
6 ounces (170 g) frozen spinach, thawed and drained of excess liquid
1 teaspoon smoked paprika
2 garlic cloves, finely minced
2 teaspoons red pepper flakes
1 tablespoon capers, roughly chopped
1 tablespoon water
6 large eggs
¼ teaspoon freshly ground black pepper
¾ cup feta or goat cheese, crumbled
¼ cup fresh flat-leaf parsley or cilantro, chopped

1. Preheat the oven to 300°F (150°C).
2. Heat 2 tablespoons olive oil in an oven-safe skillet over medium-high heat.
3. Add the bell pepper and onion to the skillet and sauté for 6 minutes or until the onion is translucent and the bell pepper is soft.
4. Add the tomatoes and juices, spinach, paprika, garlic, red pepper flakes, capers, water, and 2 tablespoons olive oil to the skillet. Stir to combine well and bring to a boil.
5. Turn down the heat to low, then put the lid on and simmer for 5 minutes.
6. Crack the eggs over the sauce, and keep a little space between each egg, leave the egg intact and sprinkle with freshly ground black pepper.
7. Cook for another 8 minutes or until the eggs reach the right doneness.
8. Scatter the cheese over the eggs and sauce, and bake in the preheated oven for 5 minutes or until the cheese is frothy and golden brown.
9. Drizzle with the remaining 1 tablespoon olive oil and spread the parsley on top before serving warm.

TIP: To make this a complete meal, you can serve this exotic recipe with pita, challah bread, or naan.

PER SERVING:
calories: 335 | total fat: 26.5g | total carbs: 12.2g | fiber: 5.0g | net carbs: 7.2g | protein: 16.8g | sodium: 285mg

SPANAKOPITA

Prep time: 15 minutes | Cook time: 50 minutes | Serves 6

6 tablespoons olive oil, divided
1 small yellow onion, diced
4 cups frozen chopped spinach, thawed, drained, and patted dry
4 garlic cloves, minced
½ teaspoon salt
½ teaspoon freshly ground black pepper
4 large eggs, beaten
1 cup ricotta cheese
¾ cup feta cheese, crumbled
¼ cup pine nuts

1. Preheat the oven to 375°F (190°C). Coat a baking dish with 2 tablespoons olive oil.
2. Heat 2 tablespoons olive oil in a nonstick skillet over medium-high heat.
3. Add the onion to the skillet and sauté for 6 minutes or until translucent and tender.
4. Add the spinach, garlic, salt, and black pepper to the skillet and sauté for 5 minutes more. Transfer them to a bowl and set aside.
5. Combine the beaten eggs and ricotta cheese in a separate bowl, then pour them in to the bowl of spinach mixture. Stir to mix well.
6. Pour the mixture into the baking dish, and tilt the dish so the mixture coat the bottom evenly.
7. Bake in the preheated oven for 20 minutes or until it begins to set. Remove the baking dish from the oven, and spread the feta cheese and pine nuts on top, then drizzle with remaining 2 tablespoons olive oil.
8. Return the baking dish to the oven and bake for another 15 minutes or until the top is golden brown.
9. Remove the dish from the oven. Allow the spanakopita to cool for a few minutes and slice to serve.

TIP: You can replace the pine nuts to other crumbled nuts, such as walnuts, or hazelnuts. Macadamia nut is my personal suggestion for a different and amazing palate enjoyment.

PER SERVING:
calories: 340 | total fat: 27.3g | total carbs: 10.1g | fiber: 4.8g | net carbs: 5.3g | protein: 18.2g | sodium: 436mg

TAGINE

Prep time: 20 minutes | Cook time: 1 hour | Serves 6

½ cup olive oil
6 celery stalks, sliced into ¼-inch crescents
2 medium yellow onions, sliced
1 teaspoon ground cumin
½ teaspoon ground cinnamon
1 teaspoon ginger powder
6 garlic cloves, minced
½ teaspoon paprika
1 teaspoon salt
¼ teaspoon freshly ground black pepper
2 cups low-sodium vegetable stock
2 medium zucchini, cut into ½-inch-thick semicircles
2 cups cauliflower, cut into florets
1 medium eggplant, cut into 1-inch cubes
1 cup green olives, halved and pitted
13.5 ounces (383 g) artichoke hearts, drained and quartered
½ cup chopped fresh cilantro leaves, for garnish
½ cup plain Greek yogurt, for garnish
½ cup chopped fresh flat-leaf parsley, for garnish

1. Heat the olive oil in a stockpot over medium-high heat.
2. Add the celery and onion to the pot and sauté for 6 minutes or until the celery is tender and the onion is translucent.
3. Add the cumin, cinnamon, ginger, garlic, paprika, salt, and black pepper to the pot and sauté for 2 minutes more until aromatic.
4. Pour the vegetable stock to the pot and bring to a boil.
5. Turn down the heat to low, and add the zucchini, cauliflower, and eggplant to the pot. Put the lid on and simmer for 30 minutes or until the vegetables are soft.
6. Then add the olives and artichoke hearts to the pot and simmer for 15 minutes more.
7. Pour them into a large serving bowl or a Tagine, then serve with cilantro, Greek yogurt, and parsley on top.

TIP: If you want to gift this recipe a more Indian flavor, you can replace the spices listed in the ingredients to a traditional Indian garam masala.

PER SERVING:
calories: 312 | total fat: 21.2g | total carbs: 24.1g | fiber: 9.2g | net carbs: 14.9g | protein: 6.1g | sodium: 1165mg

CITRUS PISTACHIOS AND ASPARAGUS

Prep time: 10 minutes | Cook time: 10 minutes | Serves 4

Zest and juice of 2 clementines or 1 orange
Zest and juice of 1 lemon
1 tablespoon red wine vinegar
3 tablespoons extra-virgin olive oil, divided
1 teaspoon salt, divided
¼ teaspoon freshly ground black pepper
½ cup pistachios, shelled
1 pound (454 g) fresh asparagus, trimmed
1 tablespoon water

1. Combine the zest and juice of clementines and lemon, vinegar, 2 tablespoons of olive oil, ½ teaspoon of salt, and black pepper in a bowl. Stir to mix well. Set aside.
2. Toast the pistachios in a nonstick skillet over medium-high heat for 2 minutes or until golden brown. Transfer the roasted pistachios to a clean work surface, then chop roughly. Mix the pistachios with the citrus mixture. Set aside.
3. Heat the remaining olive oil in the nonstick skillet over medium-high heat.
4. Add the asparagus to the skillet and sauté for 2 minutes, then season with remaining salt.
5. Add the water to the skillet. Turn down the heat to low, and put the lid on. Simmer for 4 minutes until the asparagus is tender.
6. Remove the asparagus from the skillet to a large dish. Pour the citrus and pistachios mixture over the asparagus. Toss to coat well before serving.

TIP: To make this a complete meal, you can serve it with roasted broccoli and grilled chicken thighs.

PER SERVING:
calories: 211 | total fat: 17.5g | total carbs: 11.2g | fiber: 3.8g | net carbs: 7.4g | protein: 5.9g | sodium: 596mg

TOMATO AND PARSLEY STUFFED EGGPLANT

Prep time: 15 minutes | Cook time: 2 hours and 10 minutes | Serves 6

¼ cup extra-virgin olive oil
3 small eggplants, cut in half lengthwise
1 teaspoon sea salt
½ teaspoon freshly ground black pepper
1 large yellow onion, finely chopped
4 garlic cloves, minced
15 ounces (425 g) diced tomatoes, with the juice
¼ cup fresh flat-leaf parsley, finely chopped

1. Coat the insert of the slow cooker with 2 tablespoons of olive oil.
2. Cut some slits on the cut side of each eggplant half, keep a ¼-inch space between each slit.
3. Place the eggplant halves in the slow cooker, skin side down. Sprinkle with salt and black pepper.
4. Heat the remaining olive oil in a nonstick skillet over medium-high heat.
5. Add the onion and garlic to the skillet and sauté for 3 minutes or until the onion is translucent.
6. Add the parsley and tomatoes with the juice to the skillet, and sprinkle with salt and black pepper. Sauté for 5 more minutes or until they are tender.
7. Divide and spoon the mixture in the skillet on the eggplant halves.
8. Put the slow cooker lid on and cook on HIGH for 2 hours until the eggplant is soft.
9. Transfer the eggplant to a plate, and allow to cool for a few minutes before serving.

TIP: To make this a complete meal, you can serve it with 6 round quartered and toasted pita breads, and a cup of plain Greek yogurt.

PER SERVING:
calories: 455 | total fat: 13.0g | total carbs: 57.0g | fiber: 14.0g | net carbs: 43.0g | protein: 14.0g | sodium: 725mg

RATATOUILLE

Prep time: 15 minutes | Cook time: 7 hours | Serves 6

3 tablespoons extra-virgin olive oil
1 large eggplant, unpeeled, sliced
2 large onions, sliced
4 small zucchini, sliced
2 green bell peppers, cut into thin strips
6 large tomatoes, cut in ½-inch wedges
2 tablespoons fresh flat-leaf parsley, chopped
1 teaspoon dried basil
2 garlic cloves, minced
2 teaspoons sea salt
¼ teaspoon freshly ground black pepper

1. Coat the insert of the slow cooker with 2 tablespoons olive oil.
2. Arrange the vegetables slices, strips, and wedges alternately in the insert of the slow cooker.
3. Spread the parsley on top of the vegetables, and season with basil, garlic, salt, and black pepper. Drizzle with the remaining olive oil.
4. Put the slow cooker lid on and cook on LOW for 7 hours until the vegetables are tender.
5. Transfer the vegetables on a plate and serve warm.

TIP: Ratatouille is a quite ritzy dish, you can serve it with rich clam chowder and roasted turkey.

PER SERVING:
calories: 265 | total fat: 1.7g | total carbs: 60.0g | fiber: 13.7g | net carbs: 46.3g | protein: 8.3g | sodium: 807mg

GEMISTA

Prep time: 15 minutes | Cook time: 4 hours | Serves 4

2 tablespoons extra-virgin olive oil, plus more for drizzling the bell peppers
4 large bell peppers, any color
½ cup uncooked couscous
1 teaspoon oregano
1 garlic clove, minced
1 cup crumbled feta cheese
1 (15-ounce / 425-g) can cannellini beans, rinsed and drained
Salt and freshly ground black pepper, to taste
4 green onions, white and green parts separated, thinly sliced
1 lemon cut into 4 wedges, for serving

1. Coat the insert of the slow cooker with 2 tablespoons olive oil.
2. Cut a ½-inch slice below the stem from the top of the bell pepper. Discard the stem only and chop the sliced top portion under the stem, and reserve in a bowl. Hollow the bell pepper with a spoon.
3. Add the remaining ingredients, except for the green parts of the green onion and lemon wedges, to the bowl of chopped bell pepper top. Stir to mix well.
4. Spoon the mixture in the hollowed bell pepper, and arrange the stuffed bell peppers in the slow cooker, then drizzle with more olive oil.
5. Put the slow cooker lid on and cook on HIGH for 4 hours or until the bell peppers are soft.
6. Remove the bell peppers from the slow cooker and serve on a plate. Sprinkle with green parts o the green onions, and squeeze the lemon wedges on top before serving.

TIP: To make this a complete meal, you can serve it with chicken kebabs and plain Greek yogurt.

PER SERVING:
calories: 246 | total fat: 9.0g | saturated fat: 5.8g | cholesterol: 34mg | total carbs: 32.8g | fiber: 6.5g | sugars: 7.0g | protein: 11.1g | sodium: 356mg

STUFFED CABBAGE ROLLS

Prep time: 15 minutes | Cook time: 2 hours | Serves 4

4 tablespoons olive oil, divided
1 large head green cabbage, cored
1 large yellow onion, chopped
3 ounces (85 g) feta cheese, crumbled
½ cup dried currants
3 cups cooked pearl barley
2 tablespoons fresh flat-leaf parsley, chopped
2 tablespoons pine nuts, toasted
½ teaspoon sea salt
½ teaspoon black pepper
15 ounces (425 g) crushed tomatoes, with the juice
½ cup apple juice
1 tablespoon apple cider vinegar

1. Coat the insert of the slow cooker with 2 tablespoons olive oil.
2. Blanch the cabbage in a pot of water for 8 minutes. Remove it from the water, and allow to cool, then separate 16 leaves from the cabbage. Set aside.
3. Drizzle the remaining olive oil in a nonstick skillet, and heat over medium heat.
4. Add the onion to the skillet and sauté for 6 minutes or until the onion is translucent and soft. Transfer the onion to a bowl.
5. Add the feta cheese, currants, barley, parsley, and pine nuts to the bowl of cooked onion, then sprinkle with ¼ teaspoon of salt and ¼ teaspoon of black pepper.
6. Arrange the cabbage leaves on a clean work surface. Spoon ⅓ cup of the mixture on the center of each leaf, then fold the edge of the leaf over the mixture and roll it up. Place the cabbage rolls in the slow cooker, seam side down.
7. Combine the remaining ingredients in a separate bowl, then pour the mixture over the cabbage rolls.
8. Put the slow cooker lid on and cook on HIGH for 2 hours.
9. Remove the cabbage rolls from the slow cooker and serve warm.

TIP: To make this a complete meal, you can serve it with mashed potatoes and sauerkraut.

PER SERVING:
calories: 383 | total fat: 14.7g | saturated fat: 4.3g | cholesterol: 19mg | total carbs: 61.5g | fiber: 12.9g | sugars: 10.9g | protein: 10.7g | sodium: 733mg

BRUSSELS SPROUTS WITH BALSAMIC GLAZE

Prep time: 15 minutes | Cook time: 2 hours | Serves 6

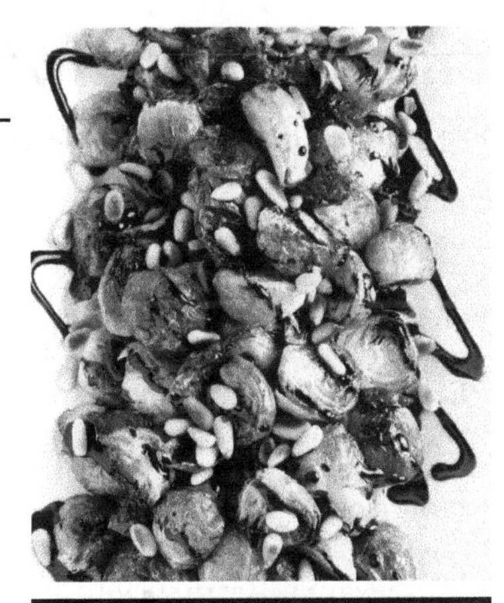

BALSAMIC GLAZE:
1 cup balsamic vinegar
¼ cup honey

2 tablespoons extra-virgin olive oil
2 pounds (907 g) Brussels sprouts, trimmed and halved
2 cups low-sodium vegetable soup
1 teaspoon sea salt
Freshly ground black pepper, to taste
¼ cup Parmesan cheese, grated
¼ cup pine nuts, toasted

1. Coat the insert of the slow cooker with olive oil.
2. Make the balsamic glaze: Combine the balsamic vinegar and honey in a saucepan. Stir to mix well. Over medium-high heat, bring to a boil. Turn down the heat to low, then simmer for 20 minutes or until the glaze reduces in half and has a thick consistency.
3. Put the Brussels sprouts, vegetable soup, and ½ teaspoon of salt in the slow cooker, stir to combine.
4. Put the slow cooker lid on and cook on HIGH for 2 hours until the Brussels sprouts are soft.
5. Transfer the Brussels sprouts to a plate, and sprinkle the remaining salt and black pepper to season. Drizzle the balsamic glaze over the Brussels sprouts, then serve with Parmesan and pine nuts.

TIP: To make this a complete meal, you can serve it with roasted potatoes, and chicken and parsnip broth.

PER SERVING:
calories: 270 | total fat: 10.6g | saturated fat: 1.8g | cholesterol: 4mg | total carbs: 38.6g | fiber: 6.9g | sugars: 22.7g | protein: 8.7g | sodium: 700mg

Chapter 12 Poultry Mains

LEMONY ROSEMARY CHICKEN THIGHS

Prep time: 20 minutes | Cook time: 20 minutes | Serves 4

2 tablespoons olive oil, divided
4 garlic cloves, peeled and crushed
3 medium shallots, diced
2½ pounds (1.1 kg) bone-in, skin-on chicken thighs
1 rosemary sprig
2 teaspoons kosher salt
¼ teaspoon freshly ground black pepper
1 lemon, juiced and zested
⅓ cup low-sodium chicken broth

1. Heat 2 tablespoons olive oil in a nonstick skillet over medium heat.
2. Add the garlic and shallots to the skillet and sauté for 1 minutes until fragrant.
3. Add the chicken thighs, skin side down, and rosemary sprig to the skillet, and sprinkle with salt and black pepper. Cook for 5 minutes or until lightly browned. Flip the chicken and sprinkle with lemon zest and juice halfway through the cooking time.
4. Pour the chicken broth in the skillet. Put the lid on and keep cooking for an additional 10 minutes or until the juices run clear.
5. Transfer the chicken thighs onto a plate and serve warm.

TIP: To make this a complete meal, you can serve the chicken thighs with roasted cauliflower and rich seafood soup.

PER SERVING:
calories: 570 | total fat: 42.3g | saturated fat: 10.8g | cholesterol: 224mg | total carbs: 9.2g | fiber: 1.1g | sugars: 2.2g | protein: 39.1g | sodium: 1169mg

CHICKEN BREASTS WITH RUSTIC PESTO

Prep time: 15 minutes | Cook time: 25 minutes | Serves 4

2 tablespoons olive oil
4 boneless, skinless chicken breasts
½ teaspoon salt
¼ teaspoon freshly ground black pepper

PESTO:
¼ cup pine nuts
¼ cup grated Parmesan cheese
1 garlic clove, minced
1 cup fresh basil leaves
2 tablespoons extra-virgin olive oil

1. Warm 2 tablespoons olive oil in a nonstick skillet over medium-high heat.
2. Rub the chicken breasts with salt and black pepper on a clean work surface, the place the seasoned chicken in the skillet.
3. Cook for 15 minutes. Flip the chicken breasts halfway through the cooking time or until browned. Set aside.
4. Make the pesto: Combine the remaining ingredients in a blender. Process to mix until smooth.
5. Rub the chicken breasts with 1 tablespoon of pesto on both sides, put the lid on and cook in the skillet for 5 minutes more.
6. Remove the chicken breasts from the skillet and serve with remaining pesto.

TIP: To make this a complete meal, you can serve it with roasted asparagus and steamed mussels.

PER SERVING:
calories: 458 | total fat: 23.8g | saturated fat: 4.1g | cholesterol: 178mg | total carbs: 2.4g | fiber: 0.4g | sugars: 0.3g | protein: 56.1g | sodium: 510mg

AROMATIC WHOIE CHICKEN

Prep time: 15 minutes | Cook time: 50 minutes | Serves 6

1 (3½-pound / 1.6-kg) whole chicken
2 tablespoons olive oil
6 thyme sprigs
4 rosemary sprigs
1 bay leaf
4 fresh sage leaves
1 teaspoon freshly squeezed lemon juice
1 teaspoon salt
½ teaspoon freshly ground black pepper

1. Preheat the oven to 400°F (205°C). Put a rack in a baking pan.
2. Arrange the chicken in the baking pan. Rub with olive oil, and loose the skin of the chicken with your fingers to form a pocket.
3. Put half of the thyme sprigs and rosemary sprigs in the skin pocket, then slide the bay leaf, sage leaves, and remaining thyme and rosemary sprigs in the cavity of the chicken.
4. Drizzle the lemon juice over the chicken and rub with salt and black pepper.
5. Roast the chicken in the preheated oven for 50 minutes or until the internal temperature of the chicken reaches at least 165°F (74°C).
6. Transfer the chicken to a large plate. Allow to cool for 10 minutes. Discard the sprigs and leaves and slice to serve.

TIP: To make this a complete meal, you can serve it with mushroom and leek salad, or roasted broccoli.

PER SERVING:
calories: 306 | total fat: 20.8g | saturated fat: 5.2g | cholesterol: 93mg | total carbs: 0.5g | fiber: 0.2g | sugars: 0.1g | protein: 29.4g | sodium: 477mg

CAPRESE IN CHICKEN

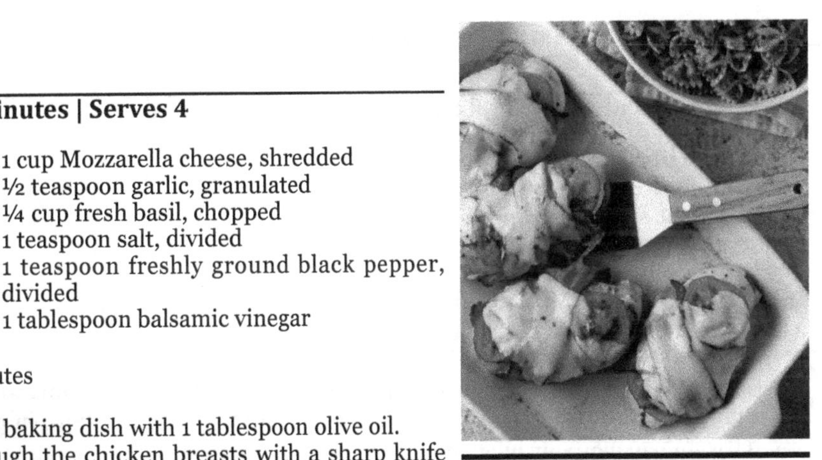

Prep time: 20 minutes | Cook time: 40 minutes | Serves 4

6 tablespoons olive oil, divided
2 (6-ounce / 170-g) boneless, skinless chicken breasts
2 tablespoons chopped sun-dried tomatoes (preferably marinated in oil)
4 ounces (113 g) frozen spinach, thawed and drained well
1 cup Mozzarella cheese, shredded
½ teaspoon garlic, granulated
¼ cup fresh basil, chopped
1 teaspoon salt, divided
1 teaspoon freshly ground black pepper, divided
1 tablespoon balsamic vinegar

SPECIAL EQUIPMENT:
4 toothpicks, soak in water for at least 30 minutes

1. Preheat the oven to 375°F (190°C). Coat a baking dish with 1 tablespoon olive oil.
2. On a clean work surface, gently cut through the chicken breasts with a sharp knife and leave the side of the breast opposite of where you start intact.
3. Combine the tomatoes, spinach, Mozzarella, garlic, basil, 2 tablespoons of olive oil, ½ teaspoon of salt, and ½ teaspoon of black pepper in a bowl. Stir to combine well.
4. Open the chicken breasts like opening a book, and spoon half of the mixture in the center of each chicken breast. Fold the chicken over and secure each breast with two toothpicks.
5. Warm 2 tablespoons of olive oil in a nonstick skillet over medium-high heat.
6. Sear the chicken breasts in the skillet for 8 minutes. Flip the breasts halfway through the cooking time or until browned.
7. Arrange the seared chicken breasts in the baking dish, and cover with aluminum foil.
8. Bake in the preheated oven for 30 minutes or until an instant-read thermometer inserted in the thickest part of the chicken breast registers at least 165°F (74°C).
9. Meanwhile, combine 1 tablespoon of olive oil with balsamic vinegar and remaining salt and black pepper.
10. Remove the chicken breasts from the oven. Allow to cool for 10 minutes, then serve with the oiled balsamic vinegar on top.

TIP: To make this a complete meal, you can serve it with braised radish and bacon, or spinach and mushroom salad.

PER SERVING:
calories: 370 | total fat: 28.1g | total carbs: 3.2g | fiber: 1.0g | net carbs: 2.2g | protein: 27.1g | sodium: 739mg

GREEK FLAVOR CHICKEN WITH SALSA

Prep time: 15 minutes | Cook time: 15 minutes | Serves 2

8 ounces (227 g) chicken breast, slice into 2 thin pieces
Zest and juice of ½ lemon
¼ teaspoon salt, plus more to taste
2 tablespoons olive oil, divided

SALSA:
½ cup red onion, chopped
1 cup medium cucumber, peeled, seeded and diced
1 (4-ounce / 113-g) cup cherry tomatoes, halved or quartered
5 Greek olives, pitted and chopped
1 tablespoon red wine vinegar
1 tablespoon fresh mint, chopped
1 tablespoon fresh parsley, chopped
1 tablespoon fresh oregano, chopped
1 ounce (28 g) feta cheese, crumbled

1. Combine the lemon zest and juice, salt, and 1 tablespoon of olive oil in a bowl. Dunk the chicken in the mixture, then wrap in plastic and put in the refrigerator to marinate until ready to use.
2. Make the Greek salsa: Mix the remaining ingredients in a bowl. Toss to combine well. Wrap the bowl in plastic and keep in the refrigerator for an hour. Adjust the seasoning before chilling.
3. Warm the remaining olive oil in a nonstick skillet over medium-high heat.
4. Cook the marinated chicken in the skillet for 10 minutes. Flip the chicken halfway through the cooking time or until lightly browned.
5. Transfer the chicken to a large plate and serve with salsa on top.

TIP: To make this a complete meal, you can serve it with fried carrot sticks and Greek stuffed squid.

PER SERVING:
calories: 359 | total fat: 22.8g | cholesterol: 89mg | total carbs: 8.2g | fiber: 2.1g | sugar: 5.3g | protein: 31.1g | sodium: 200mg

CHICKEN IN GREEK YOGURT

Prep time: 15 minutes | Cook time: 30 minutes | Serves 2

½ cup plain Greek yogurt
2 tablespoons fresh oregano, minced
Zest of 1 lemon
3 garlic cloves, minced
1 tablespoon olive oil
½ teaspoon salt
2 (4-ounce / 113-g) boneless, skinless chicken breasts

1. Combine all the ingredient, except for the chicken, in a bowl. Stir to mix well.
2. Dunk the chicken in the mixture and toss to coat well. Wrap the bowl in plastic, and refrigerate to marinate for an hour or overnight.
3. Preheat the oven to 350°F (180°C). Put the rack on a baking dish.
4. Arrange the chicken breasts on the baking dish. Roast in the preheated oven for 30 minutes or until an instant-read thermometer inserted in the thickest part of the chicken registers at least 165°F (74°C).
5. Remove the chicken from the oven and serve warm.

TIP: You can replace the plain Greek yogurt to fat-free almond milk if the Greek yogurt is not available, but remember to avoid using whole milk.

PER SERVING:
calories: 258 | total fat: 12.8g | cholesterol: 77mg | total carbs: 8.3g | fiber: 2.1g | sugar: 4.1g | protein: 29.2g | sodium: 695mg

CHICKEN KEBABS WITH CHERRY TOMATO SALAD

Prep time: 20 minutes | Cook time: 15 minutes | Serves 6

1 teaspoon lemon zest
3 tablespoons lemon juice
1 tablespoon fresh oregano, minced
3 garlic cloves, minced
4 tablespoons extra-virgin olive oil
Salt and freshly ground black pepper, to taste
1 pound (454 g) cherry tomatoes, halved
¼ cup red onion, thinly sliced
1 (4-ounce / 113-g) cup feta cheese, crumbled
¼ cup plain Greek yogurt
1½ pounds (680 g) boneless, skinless chicken breasts, trimmed and cut into 1-inch pieces

SPECIAL EQUIPMENT:
6 12-inch metal skewers

1. Combine the lemon zest and juice, oregano, garlic, 3 tablespoons of olive oil, ½ teaspoon of salt, ½ teaspoon of black pepper in a bowl, then spoon half of the mixture in another bowl to reserve until ready to use.
2. Add the cherry tomatoes, onion, and feta cheese to the remaining mixture, and stir to coat well. Sprinkle with salt and black pepper. Set aside until ready to serve.
3. Pour the yogurt in the reserved mixture. Stir to combine well. Spoon half of the yogurt mixture in a third bowl and reserve until ready to serve.
4. Dunk the chicken in the remaining yogurt mixture to coat, then wrap the bowl in plastic and refrigerate to marinate for at least 30 minutes.
5. Remove the marinated chicken from the refrigerator and run the skewers through the chicken.
6. Preheat the grill to HIGH. Grease the grill grates with remaining 1 tablespoon of olive oil.
7. Arrange the chicken skewers on the grill grates and grill for 10 minutes to browned all sides of the chicken. Flip constantly.
8. Transfer the chicken onto a large plate with tongs. Spread the reserved yogurt mixture on top and serve with reserved cherry tomato salad.

TIP: If you want a more freshness flavor to be added in the enjoyment of kebabs, you can replace the cherry tomato salad to a zucchini salad squeezed with lemon and sprinkled with scallion.

PER SERVING:
calories: 369 | total fat: 21.1g | saturated fat: 6.9g | cholesterol: 49mg | total carbs: 29.8g | fiber: 2.9g | sugar: 9.8g | protein: 15.7g | sodium: 542mg

BRAISED CHICKEN THIGHS WITH ALMOND SAUCE

Prep time: 20 minutes | Cook time: 1 hour 10 minutes | Serves 8

2 tablespoons extra-virgin olive oil
8 (5-ounce / 142-g) bone-in chicken thighs, trimmed
Salt and freshly ground black pepper, to taste
1 onion, finely chopped
3 minced garlic cloves, divided
¼ teaspoon ground cinnamon
1 bay leaf
⅔ cup sherry
14.5 ounces (411 g) whole peeled tomatoes, drained and finely chopped
1 cup low-sodium chicken broth
½ cup slivered almonds, toasted
2 hard-cooked large eggs, yolks and whites separated, whites chopped fine
Pinch saffron threads, crumbled
1½ teaspoons lemon juice
2 tablespoons chopped fresh parsley, divided

1. Preheat the oven to 300ºF (150ºC).
2. Heat the olive oil in an oven-safe skillet over medium-high heat until shimmering.
3. Rub the chicken thighs on a clean work surface with salt and black pepper, then arrange the chicken in the skillet and sear for 10 minutes. Flip the chicken thighs halfway through the cooking time or until well browned. Remove the chicken thighs from the skillet and set aside. Leave the chicken fat in the skillet.
4. Add the onion to the skillet, and sprinkle with ¼ teaspoon of salt. Sauté for 3 minutes or until translucent.
5. Add two minced garlic cloves, cinnamon, and bay leaf to the skillet and sauté for 1 more minute until fragrant.
6. Pour the sherry in the skillet and cook for 2 minutes until sherry starts to have a thick consistency.
7. Add the tomatoes and chicken broth, and bring to a simmer.
8. Dunk the chicken thighs in the mixture, and put the skillet lid on, then move the skillet in the preheated oven.
9. Cook for 45 minutes or until the internal temperature of the chicken reads at least 165ºF (74ºC).
10. Remove the skillet from the oven and transfer the chicken thighs onto a plate. Discard the skin and bay leaf.
11. Make the almond sauce: Spoon ¾ cup of cooking liquid in a food processor, then add the almonds, egg yolks, saffron, and remaining garlic. Process until the mixture is glossy.
12. Pour the mixture back to the cleaned skillet, and add lemon juice and 1 tablespoon of parsley. Bring to a simmer, then cook for 4 minutes until thickened. Stir constantly.
13. Sprinkle the sauce with salt and black pepper. Baste the chicken thighs with the almond sauce, and top them with remaining parsley and egg white before serving.
14. We finished our dish with a sprinkle of chopped egg white. Any dry sherry, such as fino or Manzanilla, will work in this dish. Serve with crusty bread.

TIP: To make this a complete meal, you can serve it with spiced tortilla and roast cod.

PER SERVING:
calories: 495 | total fat: 37.1g | saturated fat: 9.4g | cholesterol: 236mg | total carbs: 7.1g | fiber: 1.5g | sugar: 3.7g | protein: 34.6g | sodium: 351mg

MUSHROOMS AND CHICKEN WITH PAPPARDELLE

Prep time: 10 minutes | Cook time: 20 minutes | Serves 2

2 tablespoons olive oil, divided
4 ounces (113 g) cremini mushrooms, sliced
½ medium onion, minced
2 small garlic cloves, minced
8 ounces (227 g) chicken breast, slice into 2 thin pieces
2 teaspoons dried tarragon
2¼ cups low-sodium chicken stock, divided
2 teaspoons tomato paste
6 ounces (170 g) pappardelle pasta
¼ cup plain Greek yogurt
Salt and freshly ground black pepper, to taste

1. Drizzle 1 tablespoon of olive oil in a nonstick skillet, and heat over medium-high heat.
2. Sauté the mushrooms and onion in the skillet for 5 minutes or until the mushrooms are tender and the onion is translucent.
3. Add the garlic to the skillet and sauté for an additional 1 minute. Transfer them to a bowl. Set aside.
4. Heat the remaining olive oil in the skillet, then cook the chicken in the skillet for 6 minutes. Flip the chicken halfway through the cooking time or until lightly browned.
5. Add the reserved mushroom and onion, tarragon, chicken stock, and tomato paste to the skillet. Mix to combine well. Bring them to a boil.
6. Turn down the heat to low. Add the pappardelle to the skillet and cook for 15 minutes or until the stock and paste have been absorbed. Stir constantly. Pour the remaining chicken stock in the skillet during the cooking.
7. Transfer them to a large plate, then pour the yogurt over, and sprinkle with salt and black pepper. Toss to combine well. Serve warm.

TIP: To make this a complete meal, you can serve it with fennel orange salad and tomato basil soup.

PER SERVING:
calories: 562 | total fat: 17.7g | cholesterol: 128mg | total carbs: 56.1g | fiber: 2.1g | sugar: 4.2g | protein: 42.3g | sodium: 188mg

PORTOBELLO CAPRESE

Prep time: 15 minutes | Cook time: 30 minutes | Serves 2

1 tablespoon olive oil, plus more for greasing the baking pan
1 cup cherry tomatoes
Salt and freshly ground black pepper, to taste
4 large fresh basil leaves, thinly sliced, divided
3 medium garlic cloves, minced
2 large portobello mushrooms, stems removed
4 pieces mini Mozzarella balls (ciliegine), halved
1 tablespoon Parmesan cheese, grated

1. Preheat the oven to 350°F (180°C). Grease a baking pan with olive oil.
2. Drizzle 1 tablespoon olive oil in a nonstick skillet, and heat over medium-high heat.
3. Add the tomatoes to the skillet, and sprinkle salt and black pepper to season. Prick some holes on the tomatoes for juice during the cooking. Put the lid on and cook the tomatoes for 10 minutes or until tender.
4. Reserve 2 teaspoons of basil and add the remaining basil and garlic to the skillet. Crush the tomatoes with a spatula, then cook for half a minute. Stir constantly during the cooking. Set aside.
5. Arrange the mushrooms in the baking pan, cap side down, and sprinkle with salt and black pepper to taste.
6. Spoon the tomato mixture and Mozzarella balls on the gill of the mushrooms, then scatter with Parmesan cheese to coat well.
7. Bake in the preheated oven for 20 minutes or until the mushrooms are fork-tender and the cheeses are browned.
8. Remove the stuffed mushrooms from the oven and serve with basil on top.

TIP: To make this a complete meal, .you can serve it with chicken broth and roasted broccoli.

PER SERVING:
calories: 285 | total fat: 21.8g | cholesterol: 42mg | total carbs: 11.2g | fiber: 2.1g | sugars: 5.2g | protein: 14.3g | sodium: 354mg

Chapter 13 Meat

RED WINED SHORT RIBS

Prep time: 10 minutes | Cook time: 2 hours | Serves 4

1½ pounds (680 g) boneless beef short ribs
½ teaspoon garlic powder
1 teaspoon salt
½ teaspoon freshly ground black pepper
2 tablespoons olive oil
2 cups low-sodium beef broth
1 cup red wine
4 sprigs rosemary

1. Preheat the oven to 350°F (180°C).
2. On a clean work surface, rub the short ribs with garlic powder, salt, and black pepper. Let stand for 10 minutes.
3. Heat the olive oil in an oven-safe skillet over medium-high heat.
4. Add the short ribs and sear for 5 minutes or until well browned. Flip the ribs halfway through. Transfer the ribs onto a plate and set aside.
5. Pour the beef broth and red wine into the skillet. Stir to combine well and bring to a boil. Turn down the heat to low and simmer for 10 minutes until the mixture reduces to two thirds.
6. Put the ribs back to the skillet. Add the rosemary sprigs. Put the skillet lid on, then braise in the preheated oven for 2 hours until the internal temperature of the ribs reads 165°F (74°C).
7. Transfer the ribs to a large plate. Discard the rosemary sprigs. Pour the cooking liquid over and serve warm.

TIP: To make this a complete meal, you can serve it with Parmesan roasted cauliflower and sautéed zucchini.

PER SERVING:
calories: 731 | total fat: 69.1g | total carbs: 2.1g | fiber: 0g | net carbs: 2.1g | protein: 25.1g | sodium: 781mg

PORK ROAST WITH CHERRY-BALSAMIC GLAZE

Prep time: 15 minutes | Cook time: 40 minutes | Serves 2

1 cup frozen cherries, thawed
⅓ cup balsamic vinegar
1 fresh rosemary sprig
1 (8-ounce / 227-g) pork tenderloin
¼ teaspoon salt
⅛ teaspoon freshly ground black pepper
1 tablespoon olive oil

1. Preheat the oven to 425°F (220°C).
2. Put the cherries and vinegar in a food processor. Process until smooth.
3. Pour the cherry mixture in a saucepan, then add the rosemary sprig. Bring to a boil. Turn down the heat to low, then simmer for 15 minutes or until the liquid reduces in half and can coat the back of a spoon. Set aside until ready to serve.
4. On a clean work surface, rub the pork tenderloin with salt and black pepper.
5. Warm the olive oil in an oven-safe skillet over medium-high heat, then add the pork into the skillet and sear for 3 minutes to brown the both sides.
6. Put the skillet in the preheated oven and roast for 15 minutes or until an instant-read thermometer inserted in the thickest part of the tenderloin registers at least 145°F (63°C).
7. Remove the pork from the oven and allow to cool for a few minutes. Serve with cherry-balsamic glaze.

TIP: To make this a complete meal, you can serve it with mushroom and leek salad.

PER SERVING:
calories: 329 | total fat: 10.8g | cholesterol: 64mg | total carbs: 30.1g | fiber: 1.2g | sugar: 26.2g | protein: 21.2g | sodium: 387mg

PORK AND ONION SKEWERS

Prep time: 20 minutes | Cook time: 15 minutes | Serves 6

½ teaspoon ground nutmeg
½ teaspoon ground cinnamon
2 teaspoons ground cumin
1 tablespoon ground coriander
1 tablespoon grated lemon zest
5 garlic cloves, minced
4 tablespoons olive oil
Salt and freshly ground black pepper, to taste
1½ pounds (680 g) boneless country-style pork ribs, trimmed and cut into 1-inch pieces
2 onions, sliced into ½-inch-thick rounds

RELISH:
¼ cup capers, rinsed
½ cup pitted kalamata olives, chopped
2 tablespoons honey
2 tablespoons minced fresh parsley
3 tablespoons balsamic vinegar

SPECIAL EQUIPMENT:
6 12-inch metal skewers

1. Combine the nutmeg, cinnamon, cumin, coriander, lemon zest, garlic, 2 tablespoons of olive oil, 1½ teaspoons of salt, and ½ teaspoon of pepper in a bowl. Divide 2 tablespoons of the mixture to another bowl and set aside.
2. Dunk the pork ribs in the remaining mixture to coat well, then wrap the bowl in plastic and refrigerate for at least an hour.
3. Fold the honey in the bowl of 2 tablespoons of mixture, then microwave for 15 seconds.
4. Transfer the marinated pork onto a plate, and pat dry with paper towels. Run the skewers through the pork ribs and onion rounds. Brush with 1 tablespoon olive oil, and sprinkle with salt and black pepper.
5. Preheat the grill to HIGH.
6. Arrange the skewers on the grill grates, then grill for 12 minutes or until well browned on all sides and the internal temperature of the pork reaches at least 145°F (63°C). Transfer the cooked skewers on a plate and set aside.
7. Make the relish: Combine the remaining ingredients in a third bowl, and sprinkle with salt and black pepper. Sprinkle the skewers with the relish and serve.

TIP: To make this a complete meal, you can serve it with peanut and cabbage slaw.

PER SERVING:
calories: 331 | total fat: 21.4g | saturated fat: 4.4g | cholesterol: 84mg | total carbs: 10.1g | fiber: 1.0g | sugar: 7.2g | protein: 24.3g | sodium: 298mg

GREEK PORK AND LEEK BRAISE

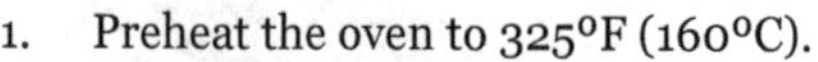

Prep time: 20 minutes | Cook time: 20 minutes | Serves 6

2 pounds (907 g) boneless pork butt roast, trimmed and cut into 1-inch pieces
Salt and freshly ground black pepper, to taste
2 tablespoons olive oil
2 pounds (907 g) leeks, white and light green parts only, halved lengthwise, sliced 1 inch thick, and washed thoroughly
2 garlic cloves, minced
14.5 ounces (411 g) diced tomatoes, with juice
1 cup white wine
½ cup low-sodium chicken broth
1 bay leaf
2 teaspoons fresh oregano, chopped

1. Preheat the oven to 325°F (160°C).
2. On a clean work surface, rub the pork with salt and black pepper.
3. Heat 1 tablespoon olive oil in an oven-safe skillet over medium-high heat until shimmering.
4. Sear the pork in the skillet for 8 minutes or until browned on all sides. You may need to work in batches to avoid overcrowding. Transfer the pork to a large bowl.
5. Heat the remaining 1 tablespoon olive oil in the skillet over medium heat until shimmering.
6. Add the leeks to the skillet, and sprinkle with ½ teaspoon of salt and ½ teaspoon of black pepper. Sauté for 6 minutes until the leeks are tender.
7. Add the garlic and sauté for 1 minutes until fragrant.
8. Add the tomatoes and their juice to the skillet and cook for 10 minutes until the tomatoes are softened.
9. Add the cooked pork, white wine, chicken broth, and bay leaf to the skillet. Bring to a simmer.
10. Put the skillet lid on and cook in the preheated oven for 1 hour until the pork is fork-tender.
11. Remove them from the oven, and discard the bay leaf. Sprinkle with oregano, salt, and black pepper to serve.

TIP: To make this a complete meal, you can serve it with roasted broccoli.

PER SERVING:
calories: 347 | total fat: 11.5g | saturated fat: 2.7g | cholesterol: 95mg | total carbs: 27.4g | fiber: 3.9g | sugar: 9.1g | protein: 37.4g | sodium: 118mg

ZAATAR AND LEMON CRUSTED TENDERLOIN

Prep time: 10 minutes | Cook time: 25 minutes | Serves 2

¼ teaspoon za'atar seasoning
Zest of 1 lemon
½ teaspoon dried thyme
¼ teaspoon garlic powder
¼ teaspoon salt
1 tablespoon olive oil
1 (8-ounce / 227-g) pork tenderloin, sliver skin trimmed

1. Preheat the oven to 425°F (220°C).
2. Combine the za'atar seasoning, lemon zest, thyme, garlic powder, and salt in a bowl, then rub the pork tenderloin with the mixture on both sides.
3. Warm the olive oil in an oven-safe skillet over medium-high heat until shimmering.
4. Add the pork tenderloin and sear for 6 minutes or until browned. Flip the pork halfway through the cooking time.
5. Arrange the skillet in the preheated oven and roast for 15 minutes or until an instant-read thermometer inserted in the thickest part of the tenderloin registers at least 145°F (63°C).
6. Transfer the cooked tenderloin to a large plate and allow to cool for a few minutes before serving.

TIP: To make this a complete meal, you can serve it with creamy roasted asparagus and clam chowder.

PER SERVING:
calories: 184 | total fat: 10.8g | total carbs: 1.2g | fiber: 0g | net carbs: 1.2g | protein: 20.1g | sodium: 358mg

LAMB AND VEGETABLE SHISH KEBABS

Prep time: 20 minutes | Cook time: 20 minutes | Serves 6

MARINADE:

½ teaspoon grated lemon zest
¼ teaspoon freshly ground pepper
1 teaspoon salt
2 garlic cloves, peeled
2 tablespoons lemon juice
2 teaspoons chopped fresh rosemary
4 tablespoons olive oil
7 large fresh mint leaves

LAMB AND VEGETABLES:

2 pounds (907 g) boneless leg of lamb, pulled apart at seams, trimmed, and cut into 2-inch pieces
2 red onions, cut into 1-inch pieces
2 red or green bell peppers, stemmed, seeded, and cut into 1½-inch pieces
2 zucchini or yellow summer squash, halved lengthwise and sliced 1 inch thick

SPECIAL EQUIPMENT:

6 12-inch metal skewers

1. Put all the ingredients for the marinade in the food processor. Process until smooth. Reserve 3 tablespoons marinade in a bowl.
2. Pour the remaining marinade in a ziploc bag, then add the lamb in the bag. Seal the bag and shake to coat well. Refrigerate for at least an hour.
3. Add the bell peppers, zucchini, and onions to the bowl of reserved marinade. Stir to combine well. Wrap in plastic and let stand for 30 minutes at room temperature.
4. Transfer the marinated lamb to a plate, and pat dry with paper towels. Run the skewers through the lamb, bell pepper, zucchini, and onion alternately.
5. Preheat the grill to HIGH.
6. Place the lamb and vegetable skewers on the grill grates, and grill for 15 minutes or until the lamb and browned and the vegetables are tender. Flip the skewers frequently.
7. Transfer the lamb and vegetable skewers to a plate and serve hot.

TIP: To make this a complete meal, you can serve it with arugula and fennel salad.

PER SERVING:
calories: 352 | total fat: 22.1g | saturated fat: 5.4g | cholesterol: 95mg | total carbs: 5.7g | fiber: 1.1g | sugar: 2.5g | protein: 31.8g | sodium: 796mg

Chapter 14 Sweets And Desserts

BAKALAVA

Prep time: 10 minutes | Cook time: 40 minutes | Serves 12

1 teaspoon ground cinnamon
¼ teaspoon ground cardamom
1½ cups walnuts, finely chopped
½ cup honey
½ cup sugar
2 tablespoons freshly squeezed lemon juice
1 cup water
1 cup salted butter, melted
20 large sheets phyllo pastry dough

1. Preheat the oven to 350°F (180°C).
2. Combine the cinnamon, cardamom, and walnuts in a bowl.
3. Add the honey, sugar, lemon juice, and water in a pot. Bring to a boil, then set aside until ready to serve.
4. Grease a baking sheet with melted butter, then put a sheet of phyllo pastry dough in the baking sheet. Brush the phyllo pastry dough with butter, then spread a layer of ⅛ of the walnut mixture. Repeat with the remaining phyllo pastry, butter, and walnut mixture.
5. Slice 3 lines into the baklava crosswise, then slice 4 lines into the baklava lengthwise.
6. Cook in the preheated oven for 35 minutes or until crisp and the edges are set.
7. Transfer the baklava to a plate and serve with honey mixture on top.

TIP: You can replace the walnut to peanut, hazelnut, or cashew for a different flavor.

PER SERVING:
calories: 445 | total fat: 26.8g | saturated fat: 11.1g | cholesterol: 40mg | total carbs: 47.2g | fiber: 3.1g | sugar: 22.3g | protein: 6.2g | sodium: 342mg

COCONUT AND HONEY CRUSTED BANANA CHIPS

Prep time: 10 minutes | Cook time: 0 minutes | Serves 1

1 banana, peeled and sliced
1 tablespoon unsweetened cocoa powder
2 tablespoons unsweetened, shredded coconut
1 teaspoon honey

1. Line a baking sheet with parchment paper.
2. Arrange the banana slices on a single layer on the baking sheet. Freeze for 10 minutes to firm the banana slices.
3. Combine the cocoa powder and coconut in a bowl. Pour the honey in another bowl.
4. Dunk the banana slices in the bowl of honey, then in the cocoa powder mixture to coat well. Shake the excess off.
5. Serve immediately or keep in the freezer for 30 minutes and serve chilled.

TIP: The banana slices can be replaced by other fruit slices such as apple slices, pear slices, and avocado slices.

PER SERVING:
calories: 187 | total fat: 4.1g | saturated fat: 3.3g | cholesterol: 0mg | total carbs: 41.5g | fiber: 5.7g | sugar: 24.3g | protein: 2.6g | sodium: 33mg

SIMPLE APPLE PIE

Prep time: 15 minutes | Cook time: 50 minutes | Serves 8

CRUST:
1½ cups whole-wheat flour, plus more for sprinkling the work surface
¼ cup olive oil
½ teaspoon sea salt
2 tablespoons ice water

FILLING:
4 large apples, peeled, cored, and sliced
1 tablespoon honey
1 tablespoon pure vanilla extract
Juice of 1 lemon
½ teaspoon sea salt
2 tablespoons olive oil

1. Make the crust: Combine the flour, olive oil, and salt in a food processor. Pulse to form a dough. Gradually add the water to the processor and keep pulsing until the dough is stiff.
2. Divide and shape the dough into 2 balls. Wrap the balls in plastic and refrigerate until ready to use.
3. Preheat the oven to 400°F (205°C).
4. Put the apples, honey, vanilla, lemon juice, and salt in a bowl. Stir to combine well. Let sit for 10 minutes.
5. Sprinkle a clean work surface with a dash of flour, then roll out a crust on the surface, then transfer to a pie pan. Spread the apple mixture on top.
6. Roll the other crust out on the floured surface, then put the crust over the apple mixture. Cut a few slits on the pie to release the air, then brush with olive oil.
7. Bake in the preheated oven for 45 minutes or until the apples are frothy and the edges are well browned.
8. Remove the pie from the oven. Let stand for a few minutes, then slice to serve.

TIP: If you want to gift more flavor for this pie, you can replace the vanilla extract to other different types of extract, such as banana extract or strawberry extract, to add another kind of palate in apple. If the nature of extract does not suit your desire for freshness, you can also make this pie with different fruits, such as pears or oranges.

PER SERVING:
calories: 238 | total fat: 10.9g | saturated fat: 1.5g | cholesterol: 0mg | total carbs: 34.4g | fiber: 5.1g | sugar: 14.2g | protein: 3.3g | sodium: 293mg

RED WINE INFUSED PEAR

Prep time: 10 minutes | Cook time: 25 minutes | Serves 2

2 firm pears, peeled
2 cups red wine
1 bay leaf
1 cinnamon stick
2 peppercorns
3 cardamom pods, split

1. Combine all the ingredients in a saucepan, and gently stir to mix well. Bring the mixture to a boil.
2. Turn down the heat to low, then simmer for 16 minutes or until the pears are fork-tender.
3. Remove the bey leaf and cinnamon stick from the saucepan. Transfer the cooked pear to a bowl. Let stand to cool.
4. Bring the wine mixture remains in the saucepan to a boil until the mixture reduces in one third and has a thick consistency.
5. Spread the pears with thick wine mixture on top and serve warm.

TIP: If you enjoy apple more, then you can replace the pears to apples, or other fruits. But the time of simmering varies from different texture of the fruit you choose.

PER SERVING:
calories: 159 | total fat: 12.0g | total carbs: 26.0g | sugar: 14.0g | protein: 1.0g | sodium: 24mg

BERRY CLAFOUTIS

Prep time: 15 minutes | Cook time: 2 hours | Serves 6

1 cup all-purpose flour
¼ teaspoon ground cinnamon
1 teaspoon baking powder
1¾ cups granulated sugar, divided
¼ teaspoon ground nutmeg
¼ teaspoon salt
2 eggs, lightly beaten
2 tablespoons plain Greek yogurt
3 teaspoons olive oil
2 cups fresh blackberries
2 cups fresh raspberries
2 cups fresh blueberries
3 tablespoons uncooked quick-cooking tapioca
1 cup water
1 cup heavy whipping cream, for serving

1. Combine the flour, cinnamon, baking powder, ¾ cup of sugar, nutmeg, and salt in a bowl.
2. Mix the beaten eggs, Greek yogurt, and olive oil in another bowl.
3. Pour the wet mixture in the dry mixture, and stir to mix well until it has a thick consistency. Set aside.
4. Add the berries, remaining sugar, tapioca, and water to a saucepan. Bring to a boil over medium heat.
5. Make the clafoutis: Pour the berry mixture in the slow cooker, then pour the batter over the berry mixture.
6. Put the slow cooker lid on and cook on HIGH for 2 hours or until the center is springy and a toothpick comes out dry.
7. Turn off the slow cooker and let the clafoutis stand for an hour, then transfer to a plate and serve with cream on top.

TIP: Before cooking in the slow cooker, you can top the raw clafoutis with grapes, pear slices, chocolate chips, or crumbled nuts.

PER SERVING:
calories: 413 | total fat: 13.8g | saturated fat: 5.9g | cholesterol: 234mg | total carbs: 67.5g | fiber: 7.1g | sugar: 3.9g | protein: 7.6g | sodium: 144mg

BREAD TIRAMISU PUDDING

Prep time: 15 minutes | Cook time: 2 hours | Serves 4

½ cup water
⅓ cup sugar, granulated
1½ tablespoons instant espresso granules
2 tablespoons kahlúa or other coffee-flavored liqueur
2 cups plain Greek yogurt
2 large eggs, lightly beaten
8 (1-ounce / 28-g) cups french bread, cut into 1-inch cubes
2 tablespoons olive oil
⅓ cup mascarpone cheese
1 teaspoon vanilla extract
2 teaspoons cocoa powder

1. Add the espresso granules, sugar, and water to a saucepan. Bring to a boil over medium-high heat. Stir constantly. Turn off the heat and mix in the kahlúa.
2. Mix the beaten eggs and 1¾ cup of Greek yogurt in a bowl, then fold in the espresso mixture. Dunk the bread cubes in the mixture to coat well.
3. Grease an oven-safe baking dish with olive oil, then pour the mixture on the baking dish.
4. Arrange the baking dish in the slow cooker. Put the slow cooker lid on and cook on LOW for 2 hours.
5. Remove the dish from the slow cooker. Allow to cool completely, then put it in the refrigerator to chill for 3 hours.
6. Mix the mascarpone cheese, remaining yogurt, and vanilla in a separate bowl. Stir to combine well.
7. Remove the pudding from the refrigerator and serve with mascarpone sauce and cocoa powder on top.

TIP: Rum is also a good choice for making tiramisu.

PER SERVING:
calories: 405| total fat: 16.6g | saturated fat: 4.2g | cholesterol: 322mg | total carbs: 38.0g | fiber: 3.7g | sugar: 14.9g | protein: 25.1g | sodium: 428mg

CHOCOLATE BROWNIES WITH RASPBERRY SAUCE

Prep time: 10 minutes | Cook time: 35 minutes | Serves 2

RASPBERRY SAUCE:
1 cup frozen raspberries
¼ cup balsamic vinegar

BROWNIE:
2 tablespoons olive oil, divided
1 large egg
½ cup black beans with no added salt, rinsed
½ teaspoon vanilla extract
4 tablespoons unsweetened cocoa powder
¼ teaspoon baking powder
¼ cup sugar
Salt, to taste
¼ cup dark chocolate chips, plus more for topping

SPECIAL EQUIPMENT:
2 8-ounce (227-g) ramekins

1. Make the raspberry sauce: Add the raspberries and balsamic vinegar to a saucepan. Bring to a boil.
2. Turn down the heat to low and simmer for 15 minutes or until the mixture reduces to half. Pour the raspberry sauce in a bowl and set aside until ready to use.
3. Preheat the oven to 350ºF (180ºC). Grease the ramekins with olive oil and arrange them on a baking sheet.
4. Crack the egg in a food processor, and add the black beans, vanilla, and olive oil . Process until smooth.
5. Add the cocoa powder, baking powder, sugar, and salt to the food processor. Process until well incorporated and lightly thickened.
6. Mix in the chocolate chips.
7. Make the brownies: Divide the mixture among two ramekins and bake in the preheated oven for 15 minutes or until a toothpick inserted in the center comes out clean.
8. Remove the brownies from the oven. Let stand for 5 minutes and spread more chocolate chips and raspberry sauce on top before serving.

TIP: Homemade salted caramel, custard, ganache are also good choices for topping. You can even top the brownies with chopped fresh fruits.

PER SERVING:
calories: 512 | total fat: 15.8g | cholesterol: 95mg | total carbs: 88.2g | fiber: 14.2g | sugar: 64.3g | protein: 10.1g | sodium: 123mg

Chapter 15 Sauces, Dips, And Dressings

FUSS-FREE HERBED OIL

Prep time: 5 minutes | Cook time: 0 minutes | Serves 2

½ cup extra-virgin olive oil
1 teaspoon dried parsley
1 teaspoon dried basil
2 teaspoons dried oregano
1 teaspoon fresh rosemary leaves
⅛ teaspoon salt

1. In a small bowl, add the olive oil, parsley, basil, oregano, rosemary leaves, and salt. Stir with a fork to combine well.
2. Serve immediately, or refrigerate for later.

TIP: The herbed oil can be made ahead and refrigerate until you want to use. The dried herbs can be replaced with fresh herbs in this recipe, which works wonderful.

PER SERVING:
Calories: 488 | total fat: 52g | saturated fat: 7.3g | total carbs: 2.2g | fiber: 1.2g | protein: 1.1g | sugar: 0.8g | sodium: 79mg | cholesterol: 0mg

HOMEMADE RED WINE VINEGAR DRESSING

Prep time: 5 minutes | Cook time: 0 minutes | Serves 2

¼ cup plus 2 tablespoons extra-virgin olive oil
1 tablespoon apple cider vinegar
2 tablespoons red wine vinegar
2 teaspoons Dijon mustard
2 teaspoons honey
⅛ teaspoon kosher salt
½ teaspoon minced garlic
⅛ teaspoon freshly ground black pepper

1. Whisk together the olive oil, vinegars, Dijon mustard, honey, salt, garlic, and pepper in a bowl until smooth.
2. Pour the dressing into a jar and refrigerate to chill until ready to serve.

TIP: For a unique twist, you can add some orange zest to this dressing. If you don't like its strong taste, just use the apple cider vinegar.

PER SERVING:
Calories: 390 | total fat: 40g | saturated fat: 5.8g | total carbs: 5.7g | fiber: 0g | protein: <1g | sugar: 5.8g | sodium: 200mg | cholesterol: 0mg

CREAMY YOGURT CITRUS DRESSING

Prep time: 5 minutes | Cook time: 0 minutes | Serves 2

1 cup plain Greek yogurt
1 large lemon, zested and juiced
½ teaspoon dried parsley
½ teaspoon dried oregano
1½ teaspoons garlic salt
Freshly ground black pepper, to taste

1. Stir together the yogurt, lemon zest and juice, parsley, oregano, garlic salt, and pepper in a large bowl.
2. The dressing can be served with a salad or sliced vegetables of your choice.

TIP: Store the dressing in a sealed airtight container in the fridge for no more than 2 days or it will lose its freshness. If you like the sweet and sour flavor, you can try add the mandarin oranges in this recipe.

PER SERVING:
Calories: 135 | total fat: 5.8g | saturated fat: 3.2g | total carbs: 9.8g | fiber: 1.1g | protein: 10.8g | sugar: 6.8g | sodium: 57mg | cholesterol: 15mg

BERRY COMPOTE WITH HONEY

Prep time: 5 minutes | Cook time: 5 minutes | Serves 2 to 3

½ cup honey
2 tablespoons orange zest, grated
¼ cup fresh berries

1. Heat the honey, orange zest, and berries in a saucepan over medium-low heat for about 4 minutes, stirring occasionally, or until the berries are tender and the sauce is thickened.
2. Remove from the heat and set aside in a bowl to cool.

TIP: Just use grapefruit zest instead of an orange to make this dish citrus-free. It perfectly goes well with muffins or pancakes.

PER SERVING:
Calories: 275 | total fat: 0.5g | saturated fat: 0g | total carbs: 73.5g | fiber: 1.1g | protein: 1.1g | sugar: 70g | sodium: 5mg | cholesterol: 0mg

ARUGULA WALNUT PESTO

Prep time: 5 minutes | Cook time: 0 minutes | Serves 8 to 10

6 cups packed arugula
½ cup Parmesan cheese, shredded
1 cup chopped walnuts
2 garlic cloves, peeled
½ teaspoon salt
1 cup extra-virgin olive oil

1. Pulse the arugula, cheese, walnuts, garlic cloves, salt, and olive oil in a food processor until everything is well blended.
2. Transfer to a sealed airtight container and chill in the refrigerator until ready to use.

TIP: The Parmesan cheese can be ditched if you want to make this pesto dairy-free. And it can be served as a topping for scrambled eggs.

PER SERVING:
Calories: 298 | total fat: 33g | total carbs: 3.2g | fiber: 1.1g | protein: 3.8g | sugar: 0g | sodium: 205mg

AUTHENTIC TZATZIKI SAUCE

Prep time: 5 minutes | Cook time: 0 minutes | Serves 2

1 medium cucumber, peeled, seeded and diced
½ teaspoon salt, divided
½ lemon, juiced
½ cup plain Greek yogurt
½ teaspoon minced garlic
½ teaspoon dried dill
1 tablespoon chopped fresh parsley
Freshly ground black pepper

1. In a colander, place the diced cucumber and sprinkle with ¼ teaspoon of salt. Toss well. Let the cucumber sit for about 30 minutes.
2. Rinse the cucumber under cold water in a colander for 1 minute, then dry with paper towels.
3. Process the cucumber in a food processor until chopped thoroughly.
4. Transfer the cucumber to a large bowl. Add the lemon juice, yogurt, garlic, dill, parsley, remaining salt, and pepper. Stir well until completely mixed.
5. Cover with plastic wrap and refrigerate to chill until ready to serve.

TIP: Cucumber is not friendly to people with sensitive stomachs, so you'd better try hothouse, burpless cucumbers if you have a acid reflux. Remember to remove the seeds from the cucumbers. The tzatziki sauce tastes great paired with grilled chicken breasts.

PER SERVING:
Calories: 80 | total fat: 3.2g | saturated fat: 2.1g | total carbs: 6.2g | fiber: 1.1g | protein: 6.1g | sugar: 3.7g | sodium: 605mg | cholesterol: 10mg

Appendix 1:Measurement Conversion Chart

VOLUME EQUIVALENTS(DRY)

US STANDARD	METRIC (APPROXIMATE)
1/8 teaspoon	0.5 mL
1/4 teaspoon	1 mL
1/2 teaspoon	2 mL
3/4 teaspoon	4 mL
1 teaspoon	5 mL
1 tablespoon	15 mL
1/4 cup	59 mL
1/2 cup	118 mL
3/4 cup	177 mL
1 cup	235 mL
2 cups	475 mL
3 cups	700 mL
4 cups	1 L

WEIGHT EQUIVALENTS

US STANDARD	METRIC (APPROXIMATE)
1 ounce	28 g
2 ounces	57 g
5 ounces	142 g
10 ounces	284 g
15 ounces	425 g
16 ounces (1 pound)	455 g
1.5 pounds	680 g
2 pounds	907 g

VOLUME EQUIVALENTS(LIQUID)

US STANDARD	US STANDARD (OUNCES)	METRIC (APPROXIMATE)
2 tablespoons	1 fl.oz.	30 mL
1/4 cup	2 fl.oz.	60 mL
1/2 cup	4 fl.oz.	120 mL
1 cup	8 fl.oz.	240 mL
1 1/2 cup	12 fl.oz.	355 mL
2 cups or 1 pint	16 fl.oz.	475 mL
4 cups or 1 quart	32 fl.oz.	1 L
1 gallon	128 fl.oz.	4 L

TEMPERATURES EQUIVALENTS

FAHRENHEIT(F)	CELSIUS(C) (APPROXIMATE)
225 °F	107 °C
250 °F	120 °C
275 °F	135 °C
300 °F	150 °C
325 °F	160 °C
350 °F	180 °C
375 °F	190 °C
400 °F	205 °C
425 °F	220 °C
450 °F	235 °C
475 °F	245 °C
500 °F	260 °C

Appendix 2: Recipes Index

Appendix 3 References

Altomare, R., Cacciabaudo, F., Damiano, G., Palumbo, V., Gioviale, M., Bellavia, M., Tomasello, G. & Lo Monte, A. (2013). The Mediterranean Diet: A history of health. U.S. National Library of Medicine National Institutes of Health. https://www.ncbi.nlm.nih.gov/pmc/articles/PMC3684452/#:~:text=The%20origins%20of%20the%20"Mediterranean,elected%20of%20the%20new%20faith

American Geriatrics Society. (2017) Mediterranean-style diets linked to better brain function in older adults. ScienceDaily. www.sciencedaily.com/releases/2017/07/170725154208.htm

Bray, G.A. (2013) Potential Health Risks From Beverages Containing Fructose Found in Sugar or High-Fructose Corn Syrup. US National Library of Medicine National Institute of Health. https://www.ncbi.nlm.nih.gov/pmc/articles/PMC3526242/

Centers for Disease Control and Prevention. (2015). Adult obesity facts. http://www.cdc.gov/obesity/data/adult.html

Fernandes-Barres, S., Romaguera, D., Valvi, D., Martinez, D., Vioque, J., Navarete-Munoz, E.M., Amiano, P., Gonzalez-Palacios, S., Guxens, M., Pereda, E., Riano, I., Tardon, A., Iniguez, C., Arija, V., Sunyer, J. & Vrijheid , M. (2016). Mediterranean Dietary Pattern in Pregnant Women and Offspring Risk of Overweight and Abdominal Obesity in Early Childhood: The INMA birth cohort study. PubMed. https://pubmed.ncbi.nlm.nih.gov/26763767/

Finley, C.R., Chan, D.S., Garrison, S., Korownyk, C., Kolber, M.R., Campbell, S., Eurich, D.T., Lindblad, A.J., Vandermeer, B. & Allan G.M. (2018). What are the most common conditions in primary care? U.S. National Library of Medicine National Institute of Health. https://www.ncbi.nlm.nih.gov/pmc/articles/PMC6234945/

Food and Agricultural Organization of the United Nations. (2010). Sustainable diets and biodiversity. http://www.fao.org/3/i3004e/i3004e04.pdf

Garaulet, M., Gomez-Abellan, P., Alburquerque-Bjar, J.J., Lee, Y., Ordovas, J.M. & Scheer, F. (2013). Timing of food intake predicts weight loss effectiveness. U.S. National Library of Medicine National Institute of Health. https://www.ncbi.nlm.nih.gov/pmc/articles/PMC3756673/

Keys A., Menotti A., Karvonen MJ., Aravanis C., Blackburn H., Buzina R., Djordjevic BS., Dontas AS., Fidanza F., Keys MH., Kromhout D., Nedeljkovic S., Punsar S., Seccareccia F. & Toshima H. The diet and 15-year death rate in the Seven Countries Study. American Journal of Epidemiology, Volume 124, Issue 6, December 1986, Pages 903–915. https://doi.org/10.1093/oxfordjournals.aje.a114480

Mayo Clinic. (n.d.). Counting calories: Get back to weight-loss basics. https://www.mayoclinic.org/healthy-lifestyle/weight-loss/in-depth/calories/art-20048065#:~:text=Because%203%2C500%20calories%20equals%20about,to%202%20pounds%20a%20week

Mayo Clinic. (n.d.). Nuts and your heart: Eating nuts for your heart health. https://www.mayoclinic.org/diseases-conditions/heart-disease/in-depth/nuts/art-20046635

Nierenberg, C. (2014). Eating beans helps lower bad cholesterol. Live Science. https://www.livescience.com/44650-eating-beans-legumes-bad-cholesterol.html

Shai, R.D., Schwarzfuchs, D., Henkin, Y., Shahar, D.R., Witkow, S., Greenberg, I., Golan, R., Fraser, D., Bolotin, A., Vardi, H., Tangi-Rozental, O. & Zuk-Ramot, R. (2008). Weight loss with a low-carbohydrate, Mediterranean, or low-fat diet. The New England Journal of Medicine, 359, 229-241. https://www.nejm.org/doi/full/10.1056/NEJMoa0708681

Thuppal, S., Von Schacky, C., Harris, W., Sherif, K., Denby, N., Steinbaum, S., Haycock, B. & Bailey, R. (2017). Discrepancy between knowledge and perceptions of dietary omega-3 fatty acid intake compared with the omega-3 index. Nutrients, 9(9), 930. https://doi.org/10.3390/nu9090930

Trichopoulou A. (2001) Mediterranean diet: the past and the present. PubMed. https://pubmed.ncbi.nlm.nih.gov/11894739/

Trichopoulou, A. & Vasilopoulou E. (2001). Mediterranean diet and longevity. PubMed. https://pubmed.ncbi.nlm.nih.gov/11242471/

CPSIA information can be obtained
at www.ICGtesting.com
Printed in the USA
BVHW091508110920
588633BV00003B/3